Paranormally Spooked: Real Encounters With The Unknown

*For my late mother and brother, and my father,
who shared this journey with me.*

Preface

In this book, I recount the intense and often unsettling paranormal experiences that unfolded in my parents' house in Borehamwood, Hertfordshire, between 1965 and 1984. The stories presented here are my most vivid memories of these disturbing events. While I am aware of many other strange occurrences, some details have inevitably faded over time. The core narrative focuses on principal stories, supplemented by reprises of others.

Those who heard these stories of real encounters with *The Unknown* were often astonished and unsettled, urging me to record them so that others could bear witness. Even highly respected spiritualists were shaken. On one occasion, a medium nearly asphyxiated. Another, when asked by a local newspaper to recount the two most serious paranormal events they had witnessed in over forty years, named two, and ours was the worst. A third refused outright to enter the room.

Later, they confided that our case was the most intense event they had ever encountered. Another seasoned veteran of spiritualism, someone who had attended countless hauntings, found our house too overwhelming to endure. Each incident is recorded here as faithfully as memory allows. Some details may have softened with time, but what follows is an honest and sincere account of what truly occurred.

As you read these stories, you will witness that I experienced encounters on both a physical and spiritual plane from a young age. I slept uneasily for many years, and I partly *lost* my late brother to these malevolent influences.

My mother was a steadfast presence and a guiding light throughout the years that led to this book. I dedicate it to her memory and to my late brother. And finally, to my father, whose continued presence was a profound gift that I was honoured to record with this dedication while the pages were being written.

Introduction

In the 21st century, we pride ourselves on knowing the world. Science measures, observes, explains. Quantum computing, crystal-based memory, and other marvels promise to reshape reality itself, changing not just how we see the world, but how much of it may still lie beyond our understanding.

And yet... some things science cannot touch. Shadows linger where reason falters. Whispers defy logic. Things move, shift, and watch, stubbornly and terrifyingly unexplained. Some events cannot be rationalised away. Some presences exist beyond understanding. And their psychological weight lingers in memory for years.

How do we confront *The Unknown* when it seems to watch us back, rising from beyond the limits of understanding? This book does not claim to answer that question. Instead, it invites you to step into the spaces where reason falters, where certainty dissolves, and where the paranormal waits, unseen but undeniable.

The paranormal encompasses experiences beyond the grasp of conventional science. It includes events that resist measurement, defy prediction, and challenge our understanding of reality. Ghosts, poltergeists, apparitions, and other spectral entities are familiar forms, but the paranormal is not limited to these alone. Strange sounds, objects moving without cause, sudden temperature drops, or feelings of a presence just out of sight are moments when the world thins, revealing another layer of existence, fleeting yet tangible.

What makes the paranormal so compelling and unsettling is its power to strike both mind and body. It evokes fear, awe, curiosity, and disbelief simultaneously. Unlike fictional scares, the paranormal is personal, immediate, and often inexplicable even to those trained in science.

Across cultures and centuries, humans have documented such occurrences in folklore, religious texts, diaries, and eyewitness accounts. Each account, while unique, shares a common thread: an encounter with something alive yet invisible, intelligent yet unknowable, and often disturbingly malevolent.

Experiencing the paranormal confronts the limits of human perception. It questions what we believe is real. It challenges what we assume is safe. It reveals how much of the world exists beyond our senses. I speak of experiences that defy conventional explanation: the uncanny, the "bump in the night," the chill that tightens your spine and quickens your heart.

These events frighten, puzzle, and compel investigation. They are not stories for entertainment or profit. They are the echoes of a childhood lived under a roof that should have been safe, a roof that hid something intelligent, relentless, and dark.

The house itself, though unremarkable from the street, was steeped in the quiet post-war normality of Borehamwood. Doors were left unlocked, children played freely in gardens, and the only drama came from the studios down the road. For the first few years, our family lived a completely ordinary life within those four walls. That everyday existence made the later descent into psychological terror all the more jarring.

We were a young family finding our feet in a time of change, unaware that beneath the surface of routine, a powerful presence had taken root. Nineteen years under any roof is long. Nineteen years under one haunted by a malevolent force is endurance itself.

This story is not only a record of spooky events; it is an account of the relentless psychological toll such activity exacts, particularly on a child slowly realising that the walls meant to protect were, in fact, the boundaries of a cage.

I was born in my parents' bedroom in February 1959. The house was an end-of-terrace property with three bedrooms upstairs, a front room and lounge downstairs, plus a dining room and kitchen. From the street, it looked like a typical post-war council house, spacious enough for a family of two in frugal, economical times. Nothing about it suggested anything supernatural.

Perhaps you have heard of Borehamwood or its neighbour, Elstree? Borehamwood lies in Hertfordshire and has grown considerably over the last thirty years, much like many towns across the United Kingdom. Borehamwood became Britain's Hollywood, producing films and shows from *2001: A Space Odyssey* to *EastEnders*.

I entered the world nameless. My parents could not agree, so my mother asked the midwife for the doctor's name. 'Colin,' she said. That was how my journey began, a journey that would uncover the unseen, the uncanny, and the unexplainable. Between my birth and our move in late 1984, my family experienced a series of paranormal events dramatic enough to rival scenes from the 1982 film Poltergeist. These events drew both the church and numerous clairvoyants to our front door.

What you are about to read is as real as the food you ate or the conversation you had today. I will provide context for each story so you can follow along and fully understand the events as they unfolded. With that said, prepare to take a journey with me – strange, spooky, inexplicable, and at times terrifying.

Time to be spooked—not from afar, but from within these walls. Welcome home, to the edge of *The Unknown*, where reality bows to what lies beyond it.

Contents   *Page*

Chapter One: 1   Mother's Dressing Table   1

Chapter Two: 18   The Tray   17

Chapter Three: 27   Saved By An Angel   26

Chapter Four: 38   The Hoover   37

Chapter Five: 50   The Church And Clairvoyants   49

Chapter Six: 58   Deadly Heating!   57

Chapter Seven: 69   Don't Let The Bed Ghost Bite!   68

Chapter Eight: 74   Spectrum Of Manifestations   73

Chapter Nine: 96   Twenty Yards Of Perpetual Despair   94

Chapter Ten: 102   The Nineteen-Year Ordeal: A   100
                       Review of the House's Paranormal
                       Warfare

Chapter One

Mother's Dressing Table

One warm summer evening in 1965, when I was six years old, my elder brother, five years my senior, and I had been sent upstairs. This was punishment for earlier mischief.

As we sat on the carpet, playing some silly game, we could hear our parents downstairs talking with members of our extended family. Laughter and conversation drifted through the house, giving the impression that there were more people there than there really were. For a while, the sound was steady and reassuring, until suddenly it changed. The easy flow of voices faltered, breaking into uneven pauses and sharper tones that rose from the dining room below.

My brother and I spoke in hushed tones about the curious rise and fall of sounds from below. We kept our voices low, not wishing to be overheard, yet the silence was so profound that even our whispers seemed muffled, almost unreal. The shifting tones below suggested friendliness and easy conversation. At times, we caught the sharper edge of argument, followed by a sudden, inexplicable quiet, as if we were the only ones in the house.

'Shoosh!' my brother said, his sudden trepidation stirring in me the first flicker of an emotional beast yet to come.

'What is it?' I asked.

He looked at me, worry etched across his face, and drew my attention to the silence.

'So, it's quiet,' I said.

My brother and I began to worry. Exchanging glances and subtle signals—the kind only siblings understand—we both wondered whether this approaching presence had anything to do with us, given our earlier mischief. The footsteps that carried our mother up the stairs grew louder, then suddenly fell silent just outside our bedroom door. Was she listening? What was she doing?

Suddenly, the door opened, and our mother stood before us with interrogative intent.

'Why aren't you two in your beds?' she remonstrated to both of us, though looking mostly at me.

I shot a glance at my brother, silently urging him to answer. He returned my look, then mumbled, just coherently enough, that he had not realised an immediate answer was required from him. His words seemed to suggest that I should bear disproportionate blame for the delay. He then added that we would go to bed shortly.

After a few more questions, she retired from the room, her footsteps fading as she descended the stairs to rejoin the family's conversation. As laughter and chatter resumed below, my brother and I continued our game, careful not to be overheard and hoping to forestall any further interruption. Unbeknownst to us, this brief, pleasant interlude was about to turn malevolent.

Some ten minutes later, we heard the door open once more, and our mother began her journey upstairs. *Was it us again? What have we done now?* My brother looked at me, and we both considered turning off the bedroom light and diving into our separate beds, but curiosity seized us faster than fear.

They grew louder, not just in volume but in menace, suggesting a weight and malice that transcended a simple human ascent. We could almost feel the pressure mounting, a silent, unspoken promise of trouble. The air in our back bedroom felt thicker, charged with an electrical tension that made the hairs on our arms prickle. It was the sound of an unreasoning purpose, a predatory approach.

The door remained closed, yet the space beneath it seemed to pulsate with the rhythm of the rising steps, broadcasting an invisible, intensely felt, warning. Every single creak was a violation of the night's peace, a calculated assault on our young nerves. Our shared terror was a silent, binding force. We exchanged a glance, and I whispered my alarm at the relentless, pulsating noise, fully aware of how formidable our mother's temper could be when provoked.

'She must have heard us!' I whispered urgently to my brother.

'She sounds really angry,' my brother said, worry written plainly across his face and echoing in his voice.

Casting nervous glances at each other and then at the bedroom door, we braced ourselves for our maternal nemesis — the final order to get to bed. Yet this did not happen. My brother and I looked at each other in puzzlement. Was this angry ascent of footsteps not a preamble to chastise us again?

No! Instead, the footsteps passed our bedroom door, letting our heightened anxiety at the prospect of immediate confrontation ebb — but not for long. My mother went into the next-door bedroom. My brother and I heard the light switch click on, then heard her move to her dressing table, which had three drawers.

We listened as if our lives depended on it, every sense fixed on the unfolding event. One by one, each drawer was violently pulled out. Because the dressing table stood directly opposite the wall between us, every sound rang sharply, far clearer than if it had been placed at the far side of the room.

'What's going on next door?' I asked my brother, whose face was etched with puzzlement. He didn't answer, absorbed in deciphering the sounds coming from her bedroom.

'God, she sounds angry!' I whispered, my voice barely rising above the charged noise. He seemed torn between investigating what was happening and staying put with his inquisitive little brother. Although it sounded like my mother, it was not quite the same—perhaps the anger had twisted her voice. It definitely sounded different, deeper, heavier, as if vibrating through the walls and floorboards, setting our nerves on edge. With every passing second, a growing dread clawed at us, like the cold, creeping sensation of unseen fingers brushing against your neck when you're alone in the dark.

For the next five minutes, the drawers were not simply opened; they were savagely wrenched out and slammed home. The old, heavy wood, rough with age, produced a razor-sharp, grating screech that tore through the wall with each pull. Every furious impact amplified the noise into a series of percussive, alarming detonations. Something was clearly being sought—an urgent, invisible pressure settled around us, palpable as physical dread. And the longer the search raged, the more the voice deepened into a frustrated, guttural snarl, escalating the tension like an unseen storm building just outside the room.

The crashes hammered our ears, filling us with dread over the cause of this furious commotion—and, more worryingly, what might come next. The feverish racket was punctuated by the scraping and shoving of clothes and objects across the table. Each new noise made me shudder in synchrony, a physical echo of my growing fear. My brother sat wide-eyed, frozen, bewildered, and not a little perturbed, as if the air had grown solid and cold around us. With every slam and scrape, the room itself seemed to lean closer, pressing in, intent on keeping us trapped within its walls.

'What on earth's going on next door?' I whispered to my brother.

My mother was angrier than ever before. Every sound—the scrape of clothing, the shifting of objects, the frustration thick in her voice—seemed to reverberate through us, shaking our very bones. It pinned us to the carpet, draining every ounce of courage we might have had to confront the furious presence next door.

Just as abruptly as it had begun, the furious commotion stopped. My mother's relentless interrogation of the dressing-table drawers was finally over. As she crossed the room to leave, each footstep seemed to argue with the floorboards, a stubborn, grinding counterpoint to her movement. We heard the bedroom light click off, her heavy footsteps pass our door, and then descend the stairs, her muttered words of anger trailing behind like smoke.

My brother and I exchanged a glance, silently gauging who could shake off the near-catatonic stupor of fright that had seized us. Even after her footsteps faded, the air remained charged, tense, as if the room itself still remembered her presence.

5

'What was all that about, do you think?' I whispered, my voice flustered and shaky, the closed door between us and her bedroom amplifying every thump and scrape we had just heard.

'As if I'd know that, you idiot!' my brother hissed, glancing nervously at the door as if it might suddenly burst open.

The suffocating silence forced the question back into the air between us, but my brother only shook his head, his eyes fixed on the door.

'Do you think she's looking for something... something hidden in there?' I pressed, barely daring to breathe, my words faltering, uneven, swallowed almost immediately by the thick, suffocating silence that had settled around us.

The door loomed before us, superficially innocuous yet hyper-charged, radiating its own cold, secret pulse. Every creak of the floorboards beneath it felt unnaturally amplified, becoming a muted, ominous drum counting down some unseen reckoning. The silence that followed her violent rummaging did not just press; it was a dense, viscous medium—a suffocating, sentient weight that seemed to breathe and wait with a life entirely its own.

Even our bedroom light, bright and static, offered no comfort. Shadows stretched along the walls like long, reaching fingers, and the chill that seeped beneath the door nipped at our necks, crawling across our skin in gooseflesh bursts. The door was no longer just a door—it was a barrier between safety and some lurking, incomprehensible presence.

My brother grinned at me. It wasn't a grin of amusement; it was the grin of ghastly comprehension, the kind that makes the hair on the back of your neck stand on end. He leaned closer, his voice a low hiss, almost swallowed by the silence itself: 'You think so, do you?' my brother hissed.

That silence did not just press; it was a heavy, expectant weight, as if the very air were holding its breath, charged with some unseen presence that coiled just beyond the door.

After a minute, we reluctantly decided to find out what all the commotion had been about. My brother suggested that I open our bedroom door. When I glanced over, a mischievous grin was spreading across his face—one that said far more than his brief suggestion ever could. I pulled the door open slowly, the hinges creaking faintly, and together we stepped onto the landing.

From downstairs, we could hear raised voices—my mother arguing with others. The tone was sharp, jarring, and completely at odds with the warmth of the family conversation earlier.

The door to my parents' bedroom was slightly ajar. I pushed it open just enough to peer inside. The room was bathed in the soft, pale glow spilling from the landing light. My shadow stretched long and thin across the floor and walls, twisting with every slight movement.

To my fearful surprise, nothing had been moved or disturbed—yet the silence felt heavy, dense with an otherworldly presence that lingered just beyond sight, as though the room itself were watching. I could feel my brother's gaze on my back, as if he expected me to shield him from whatever the noises had promised.

Slowly, I closed the door. A fleeting sense of relief washed over me, as if I had briefly escaped the manifestation of what we had just heard—though the shadows lingered, ever

7

watchful. We left it at that, our choice guided by a mixture of relief and an unshakable sense that something still lingered in the corners, waiting.

No doubt we were spooked, scared, and mystified all at once. We made our way back to our bedroom, each step heavy with apprehension, every creak of the floorboards louder than it should have been, echoing through the stillness. What could we do? We couldn't go downstairs, as we were supposed to be in bed.

What had possessed our mother to act this way? What unseen force or impulse had driven her to such strange, unsettling behaviour? And why had she neither spoken to us before nor after this second ascent? Questions swirled in our minds like restless shadows, refusing to settle.

Finally, after what felt like an eon perched on our beds, the sound we had been dreading materialised. The dining room door downstairs groaned open, slow and deliberate, followed by the soft, uneven thud of footsteps ascending the stairway.

'Oh God, this is it!' my brother hissed, thinking the worst. Each step shredded the silence. A low, almost breathing tension pressed against the walls and coiled around us. My brother and I exchanged a glance, hearts in our throats. We realised that whatever was ascending those stairs carried more than just our mother's presence. It felt familiar, yet subtly warped—heavier and stranger than usual. It was as if the house itself were crouched over the stairwell, watching, waiting for her passage.

Under more normal circumstances, we would have turned off the light and jumped into our beds, pretending we had done as asked. But we were scared; we craved understanding, we sought solace. Fear gripped us, yet the need to know was stronger—far stronger—holding us in place, as if the room itself demanded we confront what we had just experienced.

As our mother ascended the stairs, her footsteps had lost some of their earlier fury, falling into the same measured rhythm as the first set we had heard that evening. Somehow, we just knew it was her—there is a certainty in shared spaces that children understand without thinking.

Each step grew louder, drawing nearer to our bedroom, until they stopped abruptly outside the door. My brother and I exchanged a glance, our anxieties of all shades colliding within us, twisting and churning in silent chaos, as we waited for the next sound or movement.

Then, unexpectedly, she did not enter. Instead, she moved toward her bedroom. The click of her bedroom light cut through the tension, followed by murmured rhetorical remonstrations, almost as if the room itself were responding to her words. Soon, the drawers of her dressing table began to open and close with a sharp, deliberate rhythm. Some of her mutterings were clear this time: 'What's been going on here?' and 'Who did this?' The questions hung in the air, heavy and accusatory, though we could not answer them.

Then silence fell—sudden, unnerving, and viscous. But it was only a moment. Heavy, deliberate pounding soon followed, each step a malicious charge of purpose, shaking the floorboards and jarring our very chests. The sound carried a physical, menacing weight, as if the very air were tensing, preparing us for a blow. The direction of the steps suggested only one outcome—they were coming directly toward us.

Our bedroom door slammed inward, and our mother materialised before us, her gaze a searing brand of sharp questioning and radiating fury.

'Have you been through my dressing table drawers?!' she demanded, her ferocity so intense that my brother and I immediately nodded, eager to end any further interrogation.

But reason faltered under her gaze, and we blurted out in unison, 'NO!'. It was a desperate, hollow sound even to our own ears.

'NO!' she snapped back, her voice slicing through the charged air. 'My table drawers are open, and you've been through them!' Her eyes drilled into us, each word a hammer against our nerves.

'What were you looking for?' she demanded next, each syllable sharp, leaving a tremor of unease that lingered long after the question hung in the air.

With shock paralysing my mind, I struggled to think clearly. A sudden, agonising coldness swept through me, the kind that doesn't just chill the skin but infests the core, hollowing you out from the inside. Something was monstrously wrong, terribly, impossibly not right.

'But you were up here just a few minutes ago!' I blurted, the words a frantic cascade. 'We heard you! You were banging the drawers, moving all your clothes about. We heard you!'

I shouted, desperate to make sense of it—to make her see what we both knew we'd heard. But even as the words left my mouth, something inside me recoiled, as if the air itself had shifted. Deep down, I already knew the truth didn't fit. In the haze of that moment, I had forgotten the most chilling detail of all: when my brother and I had looked into her room

10

only minutes earlier, every drawer had been closed. Perfectly. Silently. Closed.

'Come look!' my mother pleaded urgently, as though any longer sentence might steal precious seconds she didn't have to waste.

But what was there to see? My brother and I had been there only minutes before and all was well, so to speak. As I entered her bedroom, my mother stopped dead, frozen in amazement. I only realised why when she whispered that the drawers were partly open—drawers she distinctly remembered latching shut before leaving the room to confront us. This shared, sudden breach of reality spooked my mother and me equally.

My brother remained a spectator of terror, hanging back on the landing. I walked over to the dressing table and pulled the drawers out further, revealing that her meticulously folded clothes had been savagely ransacked.

My mother was methodical and systematic by nature. Today, some might hastily call it OCD, but it wasn't that, she simply needed things to be in their rightful place, her surroundings an extension of her order. Her dressing table drawers, in particular, were always immaculate, each item carefully arranged as if disorder itself were a personal affront.

'Are you sure you didn't leave them partly open?' I asked, though it was less a question than an attempt to reason with the impossible.

I repeated to her what my brother and I had heard: the loud, aggressive drawer slamming and the dull thud of objects being shoved aside. We'd also heard those chilling, unintelligible mutterings that seemed to crawl through the walls. Far from easing her disbelief, my words only intensified the unsettling effect. My mother stood there, her face a mask of tense composure, struggling desperately to hold onto sanity in a house where logic had vanished.

She stared back, her expression an unblinking mask of bafflement and stubborn disbelief. The air between us was now sharply divided: her side was firm in rational reality, while mine was dissolving into spooky uncertainty. I felt a sudden, wrenching drop, realising my memory was now suspect in her eyes. It was a dizzying, cognitive vertigo.

The outcome she sought was trapped somewhere between the rational and the impossible, offering no certainty, only deepening dread.

She continued annoyingly, 'When I entered my bedroom, the drawers were partly open. My clothes had all been moved around and disorganised, as if someone were looking for something.'

The way she said it—so certain, so dismissive—made the air feel heavier. I could still picture those drawers sliding open on their own, the shadows shifting unnaturally across her room. Something had been looking for something. But it wasn't us doing the looking; that was the only certainty in the current uncertainty of what had really happened.

With growing irritation—directed at me in particular—she demanded answers. Nothing seemed to add up; assumptions blurred with fact, making it feel as if we were all losing our cognitive threads of existential reality.

I once again explained what had happened. She insisted she had not been upstairs since she had first mentioned about us going to bed. My brother, now standing behind me to my left, simply looked at me, then back at our mother.

'WHAT!' I roared.

I tried to rationalise this increasingly spooky event by recounting what my brother and I had experienced. In return, my mother flatly refuted any suggestion that she had been in the room just fifteen minutes earlier.

She bellowed at me, her disquiet sharp and suffocating: 'Do you want to go downstairs and ask them yourself?!'

I told her about the arguing downstairs, about the voices that had shifted from friendly to sharp to silent. By now, it felt like a game: who could perplex the other first.

'What arguing?!' my mother swiftly retorted.

In growing exasperation, feeling as if truth and logic had vanished for the evening, I continued to explain that both my brother and I had heard the arguing. Yet, as with all the strange sounds of this increasingly unsettling episode, it seemed the arguing had never happened at all.

My mother quickly dismissed my words, insisting that all the conversation downstairs had been entirely friendly. The looks she gave me were not merely irrational; they were sharp, contemptuous blades cutting through the last shred of my certainty.

Our conversation—which had devolved from dialogue to inquisition—was finally spent, both sides as far apart as ever. The raison d'être for this bizarre, almost paranormal episode remained stubbornly elusive. Yet, immersed in our own separate anxieties, we began to leave the bedroom. In a sudden, uncanny moment, our gazes collided mid-step as if guided by an unseen hand. We turned in unison to look one last time at the dresser, daring the room itself to retaliate.

I was last out of the bedroom and, as always, dutifully snapped off the light. The landing ahead seemed darker, heavier than usual, shadows pooling like black water.

13

A couple of yards onto the landing, we stopped. Our eyes met. Why, I cannot say—only that a raw, icy shiver crawled up my spine, as though the house itself were a predator holding its breath.

'Are you sure you're telling me the truth, Colin?' my mother asked, her voice tense, a brittle thread of sound. Her tone carried the curious, desperate rationality of someone willing to consider the impossible, if only because the simple truth had entirely deserted the night.

Before I could respond, a shockwave of sound—a deafening crash—erupted from her bedroom. It was the sound of a heavy wooden drawer violently detonating against the floor, rattling the very landing boards beneath our feet and sending a searing tremor through our nerves. My brother, his terror finally consuming him, swore and fled down the stairs. My mother and I froze, shattered and wide-eyed, silently agreeing in that moment that his panic was the only sane response left.

'We better go back and take a look,' I suggested, my voice unsteady, almost swallowed by the oppressive silence that had settled. My mother's face was distorted by fear, a living echo of The Scream, twisting with every heartbeat.

'Go on, you first then!' she said, her arm pointing me toward the bedroom door like a conductor guiding me into a symphony of dread.

The space between us—though physically only a few feet—stretched unnaturally. Each step toward the bedroom felt like moving through thick, unseen molasses, the air heavy and vibrating with anticipation.

I pushed the bedroom door open very slowly.

'What's wrong?' my mother asked, her voice suspiciously calm, as if daring the room to respond.

'Nothing… just not sure what's going to happen next,' I admitted, the words tasting of fear.

I turned on the light. The middle of the three dressing table drawers lay on the floor, tilted at an unnatural angle, its contents scattered across the carpet in small, rolling hills of fabric.

'Oh my God! What the hell is wrong with this house?' I exclaimed, my voice caught in a knot of disbelief and dread. My mother, visibly shaken, knelt beside the dressing table, murmuring fragmented words of fear and exasperation. She seemed to pray, or perhaps negotiate, with the invisible force that had so thoroughly violated her space. After I carefully replaced the drawer, she gathered the scattered clothing with trembling hands, as if restoring order could somehow erase the malevolence that had invaded the room.

Over the next few days, these events dominated every conversation in the house. Surprisingly, my mother confessed this wasn't the first time the contents of her dressing table drawers had been mysteriously disturbed. However, the drawers themselves had never been removed before. The chaos was less about obtaining something and more about provoking fear; clothing, as intensely personal items, magnified the distress.

This force seemed driven by a hostile intelligence, utterly indifferent to the domestic order it so violently invaded. Its motive felt purely antagonistic, designed to shatter their youthful sense of safety. The casual nature of the destruction was, perhaps, the most unnerving aspect, suggesting immense power and a terrifying lack of concern for consequences.

My mother also recalled that, while talking to the family downstairs, someone had mentioned an object somewhere in her dressing table. She hadn't bothered to look; perhaps it had fallen, perhaps not—but the suggestion alone seemed enough to spark this invisible search. I cannot remember what the object was, only that it held sentimental value.

In effect, my brother and I had experienced a presence that defied explanation. The presence—or whatever we had experienced—seemed to have been in the dining room, listening, then climbed the stairs with heavy, deliberate footsteps. It crossed the landing, turned on the light, and aggressively opened and slammed drawers. The entity also muttered in tones that were neither human nor entirely comprehensible, before it retreated. The arguing we thought we'd heard downstairs? Never happened. Perhaps it was the ghost's own discontent manifesting in sound.

The physical movement of drawers and clothing raised a chilling question: if inanimate objects could be manipulated by unseen force, what prevented the living from being affected in turn? For me, it wasn't a matter of *if*, only *when*.

Chapter Two

The Tray

If the dressing table experience had left you uneasy, brace yourself—there was no relief to be found in the house. The hallway always carried a heavy, unsettling presence, as if unseen eyes were tracking your every step. Cold seeped into the bones when it shouldn't have, lingering like a warning. More than once, I had felt an invisible force strike me as I walked its length, as if the hallway itself resented my passage.

Even when no one was around, using the hallway felt like walking into a cold, watchful glare. The ceiling always seemed a little lower than it should, the walls pressing in just marginally, as if it were slowly constricting its width. Sometimes, the air would drag against my clothes, thick and sticky, and I'd catch myself automatically speeding up my stride, reacting to a primal, unseen pressure that demanded I not linger in its space.

One evening, as I left the front room to walk down the hallway to the dining room, I forgot to turn the light on, so the only illumination came from an upstairs light. The lighting was dull, but just enough to navigate the hallway. As I reached for the door handle to close the front room door, I turned to continue down the hallway.

To my absolute horror, someone—or something—loomed there, barely four feet away. The form was monumentally menacing, a dark silhouette in the dimly lit hallway, towering well over six feet in height. The white of the dining room door behind it sharpened its shape like a shadow cut from stone.

Its posture was reminiscent of the humanoid robot 'Gort' from the 1951 science fiction movie *The Day the Earth Stood Still*, its arms held slightly out from its sides, ready to strike. There were no distinguishing clothes, features, or details—just a single, absolute blackness, darker than the dimly lit hallway around it.

I ran back into the front room. My shock restricted the full flow of my voice, and I must have sounded manic as I bellowed what I'd just seen to my mother and father. My mother rushed out first and shouted that she had seen a shape disappearing up the stairs.

Even with all the other aberrations going on in the house, this event made me feel highly insecure about using the hallway for at least a year or more unless the light was on when natural light was ebbing.

If I ever left the front room and the light was off in the hallway, I would close my eyes and feel for the light switch to turn it on first. On several occasions, the light was switched off while we were in the front room—and not by members of the family. Scarily paranormal!

I'd like to add something else about light switches at this juncture.

For about twenty years — from the time I was five until we left the house in late 1984 — we were forever hearing light switches being maliciously toggled on and off downstairs, especially in the dining room.

Quite often, after going to bed for the night, we'd give it ten minutes or so and then, *click-clack, click-clack*, they would start. The sound would pierce the silence of the night, making it seem louder than it actually was. More often than not, when I went downstairs, I would find the light had been put on in the dining room, so, with little fuss, I simply turned it off again. Even during the deepest part of the night, it wasn't unusual to hear this noise.

On more than a few occasions, the first person to get up in the morning later said that, on entering the dining room, the light was on, and on occasions would think I was the culprit. To those familiar with hauntings, the sound of light switches going on and off is not unusual at all.

But anyway, back to why I mentioned the hallway.

This sets the scene for what happened one evening, years after I had begun feeling uneasy and fearful about using the hallway. My dear mother had prepared dinner for all of us. I took my meal from the kitchen and began eating at the dining table.

From the front room, I could hear a programme on the television, its sounds faint but carrying up the hallway in muffled echoes. It sounded interesting so I decided to carry my dinner on a tray through the corridor into the front room, I felt a familiar sense of impending dread.

Over the months, whenever I carried a tray along that hallway, it seemed to flex subtly in my hands, forcing me to grip it tighter. At times, it felt as though it wanted to buck—up, down, or sideways—never enough to spill, yet enough to sour the atmosphere. That unpredictable, creeping interference left me tense, never knowing what cruelty might strike next.

I opened the dining room door and stepped into the hallway, dinner balanced carefully on my tray. I had barely taken a yard forward when a strange, impossible sensation prickled along my skin—something was there, just in front of me.

My grip tightened reflexively on the metal rim. The air directly beneath the tray seemed to compress, growing solid and cold, not just pushing up, but *waiting* for the exact moment of commitment. I felt a sickening calculation settle between my body and the dinner, as if the hostile entity's focus had narrowed entirely to the object in my hands, silently daring me to take another step.

Then—BANG!—the tray was violently banged from beneath, knocking it from my hands. Time seemed to slow as I watched it spin upward, the right side tilting downwards, my meal, drink, and cutlery scattering through the air before crashing with a deafening clatter against the right wall.

The food slid down the wall more gracefully, but the cup—and its contents—along with the cutlery, struck the wall and tumbled to the floor with a shattering, chaotic clatter. The drink left small, downward streaks on the wallpaper as it bled down the surface, unwillingly thrust into its new path. The tray itself ricocheted off the wall before falling with such a racket that my mother came sprinting from the kitchen to see what had happened. I stood paralysed, stunned, for what felt like an eternity, though it was probably only a few seconds.

A horrid smell quickly filled the air. I stared at the ghastly mess and ran back into the dining room, nearly colliding with my mother, who had rushed from the kitchen in response to my frantic shouting. Crying and panicked, I blurted out, 'Mum, the tray's been knocked out of my hands!'

'Are you all right?' asked my breathless mother, arresting her forward rush with such consummate ease it was unnaturally, frighteningly serene.

'No!' I shouted, sobbing hysterically, caught in the misery of this terrifying, intimate encounter.

'I told you that bloody hallway was haunted! I said something else would happen. This isn't the first time—something happened last week as well,' I wailed, tears streaming and voice breaking. 'But this... this is the worst.'

My words erupted, charged with raw, uncontrollable emotion. The paranormal hurt clawed its way out of me, refusing to be contained. We both knew the hallway's dark history, its unnatural chill, and that whatever malevolent presence lingered there—and elsewhere—was relentless. I looked at my mother; her eyes mirrored the helplessness I felt. Once again, we were confronted with a force beyond comprehension, a problem that could neither be touched nor tamed, yet demanded to be reckoned with.

Furthermore, and perhaps more terrifyingly, this metaphysical entity appeared capable of enacting a cruel directive at will. This insidious influence was designed to spread corrosive anxiety, distress, and palpable harm.

We hurried from the dining room into the hallway, where the remnants of my dinner lay scattered, a silent testament to the entity's unnerving presence.

With anger personified, she looked at the mess and shouted, 'How much more, how much more!' before running along the remaining part of the hallway and into the front room to remonstrate with my father as to why we still lived in the house. As you might have guessed, the sound of my tray and its contents hitting the wall was completely drowned out by the television.

Conflicting words punctuated the background television noise with the unremitting strength of their arguments, even if my father's was misplaced. Indeed, my mother once again positioned herself as the understanding and resolute solution to the paranormal injustice that clearly resonated throughout our house. My father seemed the antonym—reserved and hesitant, providing no immediate solution.

On hearing their argument, I felt naturally drawn to listen, hoping I might somehow contribute. Before stepping into the hallway, I cast a brief glance at the unholy mess scattered across the wall and floor. Sighing in disbelief and resigned to my inability to change anything, I pressed on. As I moved, I was abruptly shoved against the wall, as if the hallway had inexplicably narrowed to less than my body width. This malevolent presence was driving me! I shuffled along the wall, heart pounding, until I finally reached the front room.

However, my mother was now returning, so I turned and followed closely behind her as she walked back to the dining room. I stopped, though, at the spot where the terrifying event had occurred; my very senses screamed that something was not right. Inexplicably, food that had fallen to the floor was now violently smeared down the opposite wall, a hideous, impossible streak where none had been before.

The smudge wasn't merely dirt; it looked like a finger-painted sign—a grotesque piece of mockery, slick and wet, defying gravity and the natural spread of a spill. It felt less like an accident and more like a scrawl, a silent, contemptuous message left specifically for us to find.

'MUM!' I shouted hysterically. My mother spun around instantly, her expression already taut with dread.

'Look, look!' I exclaimed, pointing at the new wall soiling.

'That wasn't there, I'm sure of it—it was never there!' I cried so loudly that my father appeared at the front room door.

'Look at this! Can't you see why we need to move?' my mother shouted at my father, pointing to the soiled areas on the walls and hallway floor.

My mother supported me, agreeing she hadn't seen anything on the other wall either—after all, the food had gone entirely to my right, and the smudge was on the left. Food just doesn't bounce that far!

The air in the dining room felt unnaturally cold and flat, a silence too vast and empty to be normal. It wasn't a peaceful quiet, but a brittle, held-breath vacuum, suggesting the entity was not gone, but merely taking a deliberate, malicious pause. My mother suggested to me she'd give me half her dinner while she cleaned up the hallway mess. As she did, every nerve screamed that this brief respite was merely a staging ground for a final, catastrophic act.

Indeed, it was, as just as she mentioned tidying up, a tremendous, bone-jarring impact slammed against the dining room door. It shrieked violently on its hinges and lock, as if a bomb had detonated on the other side.

We both recoiled at least a stride, as if a concussive shockwave had thrown us back. Our immediate reaction was to rush to the door, thinking my dad had been involved outside—the sound had been that deafening, that physical.

As I opened it, there was nothing to see, just... nothing, apart from the mess, which made its presence known first by smell and then by substance. What was truly strange—apart from the obvious—was that, given the thumping noise we had both heard, the door should have swung open. Yet it didn't.

With adrenaline still raging and fear running through my body, I ran down the hallway, a mix of panic and bravado, thinking, *Try stopping me this time,* after my previous encounter with this poltergeist. Entering the front room, I found my father sitting calmly, absorbed in the television, completely unaware of the chaos behind him. Even so, I couldn't stop myself from asking.

'Did you just bang on the dining room door for some reason?' I stupidly asked my father, half aware that a foolish question would only invite a foolish reply.

'No,' came the curt response, delivered without any attempt at rationalisation—how weird, I thought.

'Didn't you just hear that crashing noise against the dining room door?' I continued, almost pleading for acknowledgment, hoping for even a hint of inquisitorial examination of my concern.

'No, the television is on,' was his second curt reply.

As I walked back out of the front room, feeling dejected by the lack of interrogation and compassion over my questions, I realised (again!) it was going to take a miracle to get out of the house. My dad simply wasn't affected by all the activity, and ipso facto, didn't really care, terrible as that may sound.

My thoughts and posture as I walked back to the dining room, oblivious to any poltergeist hallway reunion, were filled with disillusionment and sadness. It was obvious that, without my father pulling with us, our chances to get out of the house were reduced. By implication, my mother and I could expect more spooky experiences for sure.

Returning to the kitchen, my mother quickly but conscientiously transferred (slid!) half of her dinner onto another plate. I sat at the dining room table to eat, feeling guilty as I watched her clean the poltergeist's mess from the hallway walls and floor.

I got up and began to help her, but she gently urged me to return to the table and finish my dinner. Begrudgingly, I ate while she tidied. I noticed tears in her eyes. They reflected the maternal instinct to protect her child, dented yet again by something far beyond human reckoning.

Chapter Three

Saved By An Angel

Throughout the 1970s, a pervasive dread settled over our home, focusing particularly on my mother and me. My brother occupied the back bedroom, a space we both came to regard as a kind of psychological crucible, and he was transforming into someone volatile and unpredictable.

His involvement in the drug scene, something we only learned about later, amplified a core of disrespect and aggression that consumed him. The downward spiral was sharp and terrifying; he discarded loyalty, showed contempt for those who loved him, and his behaviour became a frightening pattern of erratic, sometimes hostile, unpredictability.

He began to carry an odour of disturbed things—not sweat or dirt, but a stagnant, cold scent that clung to his clothes and lingered in the back bedroom like a promise of fever. When he moved, the air around him felt strangely thin, almost electrified, as if the tension of the house had chosen him as its conductor. We were not just afraid of his actions; we were afraid of the cold, aggressive space he brought with him from that room.

One evening, the tension coalesced into pure, silent terror. While washing up at the kitchen sink, I felt him materialise directly behind me. I was paralysed by fear, sensing his presence like a physical weight, too frightened even to pivot.

Alerted by some maternal instinct, my mother burst into the kitchen, stopping just a few feet behind him. Her scream shattered the silence: 'Put it away!'

As I slowly turned round, puzzled by her desperate cry, my gaze locked onto his—eyes glazed, manic, and disturbingly hollow. The face of a man possessed. Then I saw it: a seven-inch dagger, its point hovering inches from my navel.

Had I stepped back even an inch, it might have been enough to trigger his warped mind—and end my life.

Another time, he brought home a real whip from a film he was working on. While he was out visiting, I took it into the back garden to see if I could get it to crack, with little success, I have to admit. However, my brother returned home earlier than I expected and went ballistic when he saw me holding his new prized possession. He thumped me hard, causing me to drop the whip, which he immediately snatched up.

With a sharp flick, he cracked it in front of me. I backed away hesitantly, then ran in terror towards the end of the garden, hoping the extra distance between us would make him reconsider and stop. He followed, laughing as he cracked the whip closer and closer.

Finally, cowering near the fence at the far end of the garden, I remember him continuing to crack it so close that, on several occasions, the snap made my eyes sting from the shockwave. I cried out, 'Pack it in! Stop it! Leave me alone! You're going to hurt me!' After about five minutes of this, accompanied by his almost incessant laughter, he finally stopped.

These were just two of many minor incidents my brother perpetrated against me, and I feel that the effects of the back bedroom were, at the very least, influential in shaping his hostile stance—not only toward his family but also toward others.

Sadly, by early February 1975, my brother's reckless and harmful behaviour had begun to affect my mother and me profoundly. It was a slow, nefarious downward spiral, and she broke down when a family friend visited on my birthday. My support no longer could contain her emotional crisis, fuelled by my brother's behaviour, the way it was affecting me both at home and in my school work, and her constant maternal fight to protect us both.

My mother pleaded with him to help; consequently, the family friend took my brother to the doctor immediately. They decided—and my brother agreed voluntarily—that he would be admitted to a psychiatric hospital for treatment and observation.

To deal with his increasingly bizarre behaviour, the doctors put my brother on antipsychotic drugs after he was admitted. What we all thought was a turning point in his welfare — and not least ours — was short-lived. Only three days after his admittance, with little time to adjust to a long-wanted peace, the phone rang late on Friday evening. The hospital wanted to know if he could come home for the weekend. They convinced my father, who took the call, that provided he took the medication, he would be all right. He agreed.

When he told us, my mother nearly collapsed from fright and wondered why she hadn't been asked. I just stood by her, wondering if we had moved into some kind of alternate, hateful reality. It beggared belief that my father had said yes, given all the months of incessant stress and trauma my mother and I had suffered at his hands.

A stipulation of the call—central to his and our welfare—was the imperative that he shouldn't drink alcohol while taking this medication. We weren't told why, but common sense suggested that their warning implied the outcome would not be good.

About an hour later, after the call, he knocked at the front door and was let in by my father. I should say he breezed in with a demeanour and attitude that ignited all our emotions, which were only beginning to settle after his few days of absence.

After being asked to show us his medications and explaining what he had to take, he ate some dinner but seemed keener to get back out to see his cousin. On his way out the door, I reminded him not to drink alcohol, as the doctors had instructed. 'Yeh, yeh,' he said nonchalantly as he passed me. He was on his way to see his cousin, with whom he shared a long and fruitful friendship, one who effectively connected him to a large social group.

About 10 p.m., there was a knock at the front door, his key having been withdrawn because of his erratic behaviour. I opened the door, and in staggered trouble—BIG trouble. He knew that I knew he had been drinking from his behaviour and his breath. Perhaps the drugs, food, alcohol, and cigarettes had combined maliciously. Who knows! He was definitely worse for wear, owing to alcohol consumption and the mix he had been instructed not to take. His behaviour and foul-smelling, slurred words suggested that something nefarious was afoot.

'Have you been drinking?' I asked, incredulously.

'Out of the way, you!' he snapped, forcing past me and walking down the hallway to the dining room.

29

I immediately told my mother, who remained stoic. I guess she thought it was inevitable, given his attitude and his rebelliousness toward any instruction that conflicted with his own needs. What was the alternative, trying to stop him from going out?

I went upstairs to my room, but soon he was banging at my bedroom door. When I opened it, the first thing I saw were his manic eyes. He shouted something about trying to keep away, I think, and then lunged at me, trying to strike me with his right fist. I ducked submissively, and he missed. That movement allowed me to escape from my bedroom; otherwise, I would have been trapped. I ran downstairs as he chased me, drug-fuelled, alcohol-fuelled, aggressive, and unpredictable.

My mother must have heard what was happening, because she opened the front room door opposite the bottom of the stairs as I reached it, trying to see what was going on. Observing my brother's manic chase down the stairs, she tried to intervene in what was clearly going to be a serious fight.

He shoved her aside with animalistic force and began punching me, mercilessly. The assault became a chaotic blur of pain: he grabbed my hair, dragging me along the hallway, the sickening pop and sting of roots tearing from my scalp punctuating the blows. I barely had time to writhe free before he was on me again. Through the roaring in my ears, I heard my mother sobbing, her pleas swallowed by the violence.

She tried to pull him off, but he lashed out, catching her and sending her sprawling against the bottom stair.

I yelled 'Stop it!' and 'Bastard!' until my throat was raw. Realising she couldn't pull him away, my mother somehow scrambled to the front door, wrenching it open to scream for help, desperately urging me to escape.

My neighbour heard our screams and my brother's manic craziness. The police were called, but no one came to our aid immediately. The beating continued. I was huddled on the hallway floor for protection, about four feet from the open front door. He was grabbing my hair and back, pulling me backwards to expose my physical vulnerability, hitting and kicking me remorselessly.

My mother was shouting, 'Get out, get out!'

But how could I? Every movement I made was defensive; I was, in effect, pinned to the ground.

Then, the brutal grip suddenly vanished. My brother loosened his hold, going quiet, as if physically restrained.

The air around him didn't just grow still; it felt frozen, taut with an immediate, overwhelming force that pressed him flat against the hallway wall very close to the front room door, holding him there like a struggling insect pinned under glass. He gasped, not from exhaustion, but from the sudden, profound lack of control. Simultaneously, I felt the unmistakable sensation of two gentle pressures closing beneath my armpits, firm yet oddly dense, like hands formed from solidified air.

As he seemed to be pinned against the wall, I was lifted in a way that defied physics, a weightlessness akin to the momentary *zero gravity* of a parabolic flight, yet entirely benevolent.

With the pressure formed beneath my armpits, a sudden, powerful whoosh occurred, I was propelled out of the front door and onto the concrete path. I flew upward by perhaps two feet and outward by five, landing miraculously on my feet without a stumble. The momentum, the force, the instantaneous liberation—it was a movement born not of human strength, but of extraordinary, targeted intervention.

I turned round and my mother was shouting, 'Go, go, and don't come back in!'

My brother was breathing heavily, sweating profusely, snorting, evil-eyed, and seemingly pumping steam through his nostrils like some character out of a cartoon. Blood was on his hands; my head felt like a punchbag, and my ribs ached. He moved toward me, and incredibly, I moved toward him. We stood facing each other across the front doorstep, like two boxing pugilists before a fight. Was I really going back in? Was stupidity my middle name? I remember moving forward, but it felt as if an invisible barrier held me back from crossing the doorstep.

'Want some more?' my brother asked menacingly, his words delivered with a threatening, almost malignant tone that carried far more weight of potential harm than the words alone could convey.

Distracted by my own distraught state, and by my mother sobbing at the bottom of the stairs, I shouted to her, 'What about you, Mum?'

'Just go,' she cried, collapsing further into tears.

My brother looked around at her. For a moment, I feared he might turn on her as well, but instead, he simply stared back at me, eyes wild and unrelenting. Rather than accept his unspoken challenge for a second round, as I had already suffered a technical knockout in the first, common sense prevailed, and I walked away towards the front gate. I expected him to chase me, but he remained where he was, watching his prey retreat. I glanced back at my mother, crying uncontrollably, and at my brother, who seemed utterly elsewhere, lost in his own violent world.

I went to the next-door neighbour, who was standing at his front door, fully aware of everything that had happened.

'I've called the police. Are you alright?' he asked. Nothing seemed alright. I don't remember much else of what was said; everything felt a bit hazy, as you'd expect.

However, I ran round to my Auntie's, who lived just minutes away, and stayed there briefly. Shaking uncontrollably from head to toe, I was told by my Auntie to sit by the open coal fire, whose glowing warmth and radiant heat offered comfort. As I settled, thoughts spiralled through my mind about what had just happened. Becoming aware of blood on my temples, I slowly and distressingly pulled clumps of my hair from my scalp, roots attached and bloodied. Then, I threw them onto the fire, watching them sizzle and burn.

After about thirty minutes, I returned home to find my uncle and the police in attendance. They arrested my brother and asked my mother if she wanted to press charges. Unbelievably, she said no. She was not in a good place at the time—mentally, emotionally, or physically—but I remained profoundly grateful to her for what she had done.

Later, when the jagged edges of trauma had receded slightly, we spoke about the incident. I turned to her and said, 'Mum, what you did was amazing given the circumstances.'

She looked at me then, an angelic clarity on her face, and responded with gentle finality, 'I never helped you at all.' Perplexed, I laughed a short, strained laugh. 'But you did. I felt your hands lift me and throw me out,' I insisted, struggling to anchor the truth in common sense.

Her compassionate gaze intensified, and she repeated the phrase, as if etching it into my soul: 'I never helped you.'

She leaned forward. 'I couldn't. I was slumped at the bottom of the stairs, in shock and pain, watching your brother hit you.'

She continued, the awe in her voice palpable, 'Then I saw him simply pushed away from you. You were lifted up by something and literally hurled out the door. Your arms didn't move—they just dangled, as if strong, invisible hands were under your arms.'

Such was my misdirection of causation in that moment that I felt dizzy, trying to unpack what was real and what was not. I suddenly said, 'I remember your hands under my arms, and then you lifted and pushed me forward.'

But no—my mother's response was once again clear and concise. This was nothing existential about my escape; it suggested something more spiritual, perhaps even divine, in nature.

Now, writing this after many years of reflection, I can tell you exactly what happened. First, I remember feeling my brother loosen his grip on me and go quiet, as if surprised or distracted by something. Then he moved to my right, seemingly pinned against the hallway wall adjoining the front room.

As this happened, I felt pressure under my arms and beneath me in general. Then, with a sudden *whoosh*, I was propelled out of the front door, thrown upward by about two feet and outward by some five feet onto the concrete path outside. The force was accompanied by an overwhelming feeling that was entirely benevolent—otherwise, I would surely mention it here.

When recalling this infamous incident some three years later, my brother said he felt inexplicably pushed away and held back. He couldn't understand how, which supported my mother's interpretation of events. More worryingly, he admitted he felt driven to hurt and was 'just out of it.' This may have been true.

After I escaped, he bizarrely calmed down, became rational within minutes according to my mother, and was quite lucid. Were good and evil forces playing out in our hallway that night? Who knows. If so, good clearly defeated evil.

Accordingly, at that time, I dared to believe I had been saved by an angel, perhaps my guardian angel. I promised myself that I would be forever grateful to whoever it was and that perhaps, one day, I would have the chance to say thank you in person. My mother said I had been blessed that night to be touched and even thrown by spirit in a truly unique way. Had such intervention not occurred, who knows what might have happened. I am and always will be profoundly grateful.

Later in the year, in July 1975, I decided to seek a reading from a respected clairvoyant whom my mother had consulted several times over many years. They had become good friends. This incident had not been relayed to the clairvoyant because my mother's preoccupations lay elsewhere, and one of those, I think, you could probably guess.

It was never indifference or lack of concern that prevented her from telling the story. Rather, it was deeply personal, and her emotions were still too raw for public consumption. No doubt the clairvoyant did not need to be told anyway.

But back to what happened when I went for my reading, which was my very first of any kind.

I arrived on time at the clairvoyant's house and was greeted with a smile. She briefly praised my mother, which was very nice. During the reading, she mentioned a number of pertinent things before moving on to the events of that fateful February night.

She explained that a higher authority had intervened with my guides. This was highly unusual and would not have happened without that authority's permission. She mentioned a few other details as well. The words blessed and angel were inextricably linked to the incident before she shifted the focus to immediate career plans and spirituality in general.

Remarkably, in the same reading, she correctly predicted our house move, which at the time sounded very strange. The first prediction was that the move would be within Borehamwood and would not occur for several years, which turned out to be correct. At the time of the prediction, this seemed odd because my parents had expected to move farther afield; most of the interest in property and potential moves had come from outside the local area. Yet at the same time, they still wanted to remain close to family and friends, creating a confusing tension in their plans.

The second prediction was that the move would not occur for at least another seven years, which also proved accurate, as we finally relocated in late 1984. This prediction was equally surprising because we had wanted to move immediately.

Chapter Four

The Hoover

Of all the incidents that occurred in our home, this was by far the most paranormally significant—reminiscent of a scene from a Hollywood horror film like *Poltergeist*. Objects moved seemingly on their own, physical and emotional damage intertwined, and strange, unsettling odours permeated the air. All these factors combined in a way that suggested a profoundly malevolent presence at work.

Back in 1978, at age nineteen, I was working for an international bank in Brighton, East Sussex. At the time, my father was on night shifts in London. As a result, my mother was often alone during the hours when we are perhaps most vulnerable. The stillness of the night seemed to amplify every unexpected sound, feeding anxiety and encouraging the false sense of security found in hiding beneath the bedcovers.

Given the house had a history of insalubrious sounds— light switches being switched on and off in a manic, frenzied way, creaking doors slowly opening, sudden breathing heard from nowhere, and objects moving seemingly on their own—it was unsurprising that my mother felt vulnerable to the malevolent whims of paranormal harassment. Bed linen being pulled or tugged, and the usual things that go bump in the night, only added to her unease.

Into this unsettling mix, I would visit my parents at the weekend. My visits were primarily to break the cycle of my mother being alone and exposed to these disturbances. I also went in response to her requests, as she felt defenceless against the lurking dangers we were both acutely aware of. Each visit was an attempt to provide some measure of comfort and protection in a house that often seemed anything but safe.

Before I describe the incident, it's important to explain the layout of our house. The door from the front room opened into the hallway. Directly opposite this door stood a sturdy hoover box, roughly two feet high, supporting a cylinder hoover with its vacuum pipe stored inside.

The hoover itself was just over two feet long and heavy enough to require some effort to lift. The hoover box was stable, and when the hoover was placed on it, there was no reason to suspect it could fall off it. The straight-line distance from the hoover to the front room door was approximately five feet.

During one weekend visit, just as the clock ticked past midnight into Saturday morning, my mother and I were sitting in the front room talking. The night was quiet, the kind of stillness that makes every little sound feel amplified. Then, barely fifteen minutes into the new day, a tremendous crash struck the front door, rattling it violently on its hinges, as if some enraged person had struck it with unimaginable force.

Can you imagine it—sitting there, chatting in the calm of the night, when suddenly a deafening thump shatters the silence? With my father at work and no one else in the house, the sound was deeply unnerving, sparking a rush of pure, raw dread. 'What was that?' I exclaimed, my voice trembling. The shock hit me full force, as if someone had crept up behind me and violently shattered the silence.

For a few minutes, my mother and I just stared at each other, jaws dropped, hearts pounding, seized by a petrifying paralysis. We didn't exchange another word, simply waiting, listening, wondering what might happen next. I half expected burglars to burst in through the door—or even the windows.

At a moment like that, your mind races uncontrollably, imagining all kinds of dangers. After a few minutes of shared, nervous deliberation, we slowly rose and edged toward the front room door.

'Go on, you look,' my mother urged, her voice calm but encouraging. Just like in an old movie, she was right behind me, offering silent support. I pressed my face to the window first, scanning the area for any signs of a break-in, but all was eerily still.

Reluctantly, I moved closer, knowing I had to open the door to uncover the source of the noise. About two feet away, I froze. From the other side, I thought I could hear something—shuffling, the faint rustle of objects or paper. My heart pounded. God, I was terrified!

What scariness lay behind that door? I moved my right hand toward the front room door handle and placed it on it. Just as I did, something happened that unintentionally shook my focus. From behind, I heard a voice.

'Go on, open it, Colin,' said my mother, who was clearly trying to act vicariously through me—bless her.

I thought that if I opened the door quickly, I might take whoever was outside in the hallway by surprise. Yes, I know—idiocy personified! So, without further apprehension, I pulled the door open as quickly as I could, summoning all the courage I had to confront whoever lay beyond it. I must have opened it with such speed that the resultant gust of wind blew past me, momentarily lifting most of my hair.

Opening the door quickly, I was startled to see what had caused the loud, sinister thump against the front room door. It was the cylinder hoover, lying at a slight angle and almost touching the door. The six-foot hoover pipe lay nearby, having become detached from the hoover's front. Dirt had billowed out from the open hoover, smothering about a foot of carpet next to the door.

'It's the hoover… but how?' I exclaimed, relieved.

Somehow, the hoover had managed to fly across five feet of hallway and strike the door about two feet from the ground, leaving a noticeable indentation. Residue from the impact was scattered on the hallway floor directly below, consisting of tiny fragments of wood and flecks of paint.

Apprehensively yet resolutely, I reached out with my right hand toward the hoover, half-expecting it to spring to life and fly at me again. After convincing myself that it would not, I picked it up and carefully placed it back on the box, pipe included, as though returning a wayward animal to its designated home.

I then noticed the newspaper rack next to the hoover box.

'Oh my God! The newspapers, the letters—they're all over the place!' I exclaimed, distressed, as my mother nervously gripped the back of my jersey.

The newspapers had been violently rifled through—some toppled across the floor, others teetering precariously from the rack. Torn letters lay strewn among them, disordered and crumpled, as if tossed by invisible hands. I swallowed hard and let out a nervous sigh, my eyes scanning the chaotic scene as a cold shiver of revulsion ran down my spine.

40

The air was no longer just cold; it felt heavy, viscous, pressing against the skin like a shroud. This presence was not passive; it was gloating. The chaotic mess on the floor seemed to shimmer and writhe in the hallway light, a stage set for deliberate psychological warfare, each scattered scrap a testament to the entity's contempt for our order, our privacy, and our sense of sanctuary.

If this wasn't bad enough, I became aware of something so awful, so sinister, that the hairs on the back of my neck stood on end, and all my senses screamed danger. Something was there. It was watching me—watching us—like a powerful, stealthy predator sizing up its prey. The thought that I could be the next flying victim overwhelmed my mind.

What was it? The subjective dread became almost existential as a pungent smell of sulphur suddenly overpowered me. My mother, who was clearly in a 'help us' mode, commented as well, and we both went from scared to a state of overwhelming, primal terror.

The stench was overwhelming. We knew we could not leave the situation as it was and required urgent spiritual assistance. The 1984 paranormal film *Ghostbusters* comes to mind now as I reflect; if such a service had existed (and the film had not been made then), that glitzy ambulance with its distinctive siren would surely have been called.

Instead, we contacted a local clairvoyant, who ran the nearby spiritualist centre. Although not ordained, he held a junior religious qualification, and at the time he represented the best immediate source of spiritual help/guidance we could access.

The problem arose as I tried to pick up the telephone handset, located next to the replaced hoover. Suddenly, the handset was knocked from my hand, first striking the wall and then falling down the narrow space between the newspaper rack and the wall. In shock, my mother and I bolted into the dining room. Almost in synchrony, we turned and looked down the hallway. Small papers were being slightly moved, as if a mild wind had manifested in the very space we had just occupied.

Overcome by the sheer intensity of the moment, the words burst out before I could stop them.

'No way! Did you see that—the bloody telephone was knocked right out of my hand?!' I shouted at my mother, who by this time was lost for words in consternation.

'But I've got to ring him!' I cried desperately. 'Come on, we must make this call. Let's try again!'

I returned to the telephone, feeling isolated, inadequate, and helpless. As we walked down the hallway and the telephone came into view from behind the stairway railings, my thoughts raced: what if something else happens? The sense of foreboding was almost toxic.

As I placed my hand on the handset to pick it up, I was immediately struck by how cold it was—unusually cold. This in itself was abnormal, especially since only moments before it had felt completely normal. Evidently, something was manifest there and had not departed. The hallway was also cold, although the awful smell from earlier was no longer present. The handset's chill made me recoil, and I replaced it so quickly that it only served to frighten my mother further.

'What's wrong?' my mother asked nervously.

'It's freezing cold,' I replied.

'Just phone him, please,' my mother implored.

I looked at my mum, who was gesturing emphatically, urging me to pick the handset back up and continue.

'What the hell was that?' I shouted as we both cowered and trembled in shock. A huge, unearthly noise—somewhere between a thud and a bang—erupted from the back bedroom, traveling with ballistic, spine-chilling precision that assaulted our senses.

We were both in a state of spiritual disarray from the paranormal happenings of the past few hours, and this only sent our nerves stratospheric. My mother walked along the hallway, and we both stared up the stairway as if expecting something to appear. I looked away, my thoughts returning to the urgent need to telephone the spiritualist.

The air on the stairway itself felt static, charged with something unknown. Though the hallway light illuminated the lower steps, the upper steps and the landing remained bathed in semi-darkness, because we were too anxious to reach the hallway switch to turn the landing light on. This deep shadow felt like a thick, rough velvet curtain hanging over the top steps. Every instinct warned that crossing that threshold meant stepping into a dimension where the rules of the house, and sanity, no longer applied. We wanted to turn the light on and expose, reveal whatever we felt was menacingly looking at us.

'Oh my God!' chillingly said my mother.

I looked round at her; she looked terrified. What the hell was my mother looking at? Yet, her statement, made so eerily, unnerved me even more, and I froze for what seemed like an eternity. Her terrified countenance sent chills through me, whilst my hair literally rose on the back of my neck. I actually feared to look up the stairway, because if I did, it would be at whatever had made my mother make that nervous exclamation in the first place.

However, look round I did. It was indeed an 'Oh my God!' moment. As we both looked and squinted our eyes in palpable disbelief towards the top of the stairway, we saw something. The light from the downstairs hallway provided only partial illumination, and yet this dark, central mass seemed to swallow even that.

It had no discernible shape—not a circle, but an irregular, heavy concentration of blackness—a hole in our reality. It hung there for a few seconds that felt like an eternity before, slowly and deliberately, it slid silently to the right, towards the back bedroom. We remained frozen, continuing to stare into the semi-darkness as if expecting a paranormal encore.

We were physically incapable of speech. My mother and I spoke very few words during this ordeal, utterly numbed by it all.

Yet we did act on our fears. We walked briskly back to the dining room, uncertain whether to break down in terror or to be brave and make the telephone call to the clairvoyant. Our conversation was brief, but I will leave it to your imagination as to what might have been said under such paranormal circumstances. Needless to say, expletives, fear, concern, and utter bewilderment filled both our thoughts and our words.

That telephone call had to be made, now more than ever. If we had ever needed divine inspiration, it was at this moment. I cannot say whether such inspiration arrived. In any case, five minutes after our hurried return to the dining room, we mustered the courage to walk back down the hallway and try once more.

I picked up the handset again (yes, it was still unusually cold) and tried to ring the clairvoyant, only to be met with crackling on the line and no dial tone.

'Bloody thing won't work now!' I shouted, half-expecting the telephone to miraculously fix itself.

We felt so uneasy standing there in the hallway, where the spooky gravitas had just reached its zenith. Eventually, I got through to the clairvoyant and spoke to him, my voice trembling with fear. I'm sure it sounded peculiar—not just because of my tone, but because the words seemed to spill from my mouth in a nonsensical rush. He said he'd be about 25 minutes, so during this time, my mother and I once again returned to the dining room to continue our stilted and nervous conversation about what had happened and what was yet to come.

The air in the dining room offered no solace; it felt too still, too sterile, as if the darkness in the hallway outside had leached the very warmth and sound from our sanctuary. The seconds stretched into heavy, uneven minutes, each one magnifying the fear that the entity was silently, malevolently watching us, testing the boundaries of our temporary refuge before making its next aggressive move.

Indeed, we heard some faint movement in the hallway and saw papers move slightly around as if some breeze had occurred... but we refused to investigate further until help arrived—which it did, announced by a loud knock at the front door. I opened it, and in walked our clairvoyant, hopefully the nemesis of whatever poltergeist had been tormenting us.

We led him along the hallway to the dining room and began recounting the events. He stood quietly, listening as my mother and I tried to rapidly explain our recent paranormal experiences in a manner barely resembling normal conversation. As we laid bare what had happened in the hallway, he showed initial signs of surprise, soon replaced by trepidation and consternation as the full scale of the events became clear.

In any case, after fifteen minutes he returned to the scene of the incident. Speaking to us from the hallway, he said, 'There is an evil entity here that must be removed.' My mother and I were no novices in these matters; this clairvoyant was a respected medium and founder of the local Spiritualist Centre, which still operates today. He then asked one of us to stand beside him in the hallway while he recited a prayer.

'Is that truly necessary?' I boomed, hesitant, from the dining room.

'Absolutely necessary,' he affirmed, his voice allowing no debate. I drew the short straw but did not want to go. Reluctantly, I walked along the hallway from the dining room and stood beside him and the offending objects of the moment—the hoover and the telephone. The spiritualist placed some small religious regalia on them and asked if it was all right to begin praying.

'Yes!' I replied nervously. But just then he paused and gave me an important caveat.

'Now, whatever happens, I will continue the prayer, and you must stay calm,' he instructed firmly.

'But what if something goes wrong?' I asked hesitantly, my worry evident.

46

'Let's hope not,' he answered.

No sooner had he started the prayer than I shouted, 'It's back!' The strong smell of sulphur returned with a vengeance. It was no good—I couldn't take this.

'I'm going back!' I remonstrated with the clairvoyant, beginning to retreat toward the dining room.

'No, stay here,' he replied quickly and forcefully, holding out his right arm to restrain me.

With my egress from the hallway temporarily held in abeyance by his arm, I pleaded with him to stop the prayer, but he refused. I wanted to run, and I knew staying there was the definitive stand needed to restore some peace to our house at that moment in time.

'We must complete this—it has to be done!' he shrieked, as the tension ratcheted up several notches.

It felt as though the *Twilight Zone* had taken up residence in our house. This was no mere imagination. Within seconds of the clairvoyant beginning the prayer, I felt something hovering close—powerful, devious, and menacing. I shivered; my heart pounded with agonising terror—fear of that menacing presence, and a profound, existential dread of *The Unknown*.

As he continued the prayer, the smell of sulphur grew ever more potent, seeming to envelop my very senses, though not, I hasten to add, my being. Once the prayer was completed and the sulphurous stench dissipated, I retreated with a walking gait—if such a thing is possible—back to the dining room, where my mother watched on, thankful to be merely a spectator to it all.

The clairvoyant finally left at around 2.15 a.m., assuring us that if any further problems arose, he would return post-haste.

Evidently, we had witnessed genuine poltergeist activity. It displayed enough energy to lift a hoover and hurl it five feet across the hallway, crashing it into our front room door. The impact damaged both the hoover, which was solidly made, and the robust door, leaving noticeable dents. The hoover pipe, papers, and letters were also displaced, scattered by some unseen force.

The strong smell of sulphur was a stark sign of evil. And, looming over it all, there was the dark, malevolent presence at the top of the stairway. It may have caused the earlier bang and even knocked the telephone from my hand.

How would you have reacted to this? Remember, there were no mobile phones or social networks back then; it was past midnight, and there was no one to call for help—certainly not for what had just happened. And what could we even say? If we had phoned the police, we would likely have been laughed at, perhaps even accused of wasting their time. These paranormal episodes, individually or together, seemed straight out of the movie *Poltergeist*. All the elements were there—and, unfortunately, so were my mother and I.

Chapter Five

The Church And Clairvoyants

By the mid-seventies, the spookiness had become so frequent that we had heated, lengthy, and at times troubling discussions about it. Eventually, we decided to seek advice from local church representatives regarding the possibility of having the house blessed. My mother visited them several times concerning a blessing, though she never spoke at length about it.

At that time, such matters were not something one casually reported, and certainly not something that warranted summoning the church to your front door. Reports of paranormal activity were largely considered taboo.

Any visit also raised the crucial question of whether it might merely exacerbate an already volatile situation rather than pacify it.

The prevailing sentiment, derived from church protocols, was one of reluctance to approve such a visit. My mother was told that the church did not undertake such blessings lightly, and that any blessing would be formally recorded, along with the reasons for it, for future reference. She was also required to document why the blessing was justified.

In recognition of her quiet determination—or 'judicious persistence,' if one prefers a more formal phrasing—she was eventually granted a visit from the local vicar to bless our house.

My poor mother was at her wits' end—with me not far behind—over all the happenings in the house. Yet, counterintuitively, and diametrically opposed to our awareness of these ongoing spooky events, my father seemed largely unconcerned, going along in the hope that my mother would quieten down. We all had to be present for the house to be blessed by our local vicar.

On the appointed day, he arrived in his traditional vestments and donned a stole. Moving from room to room, he blessed the house, shaking his aspergillum to sprinkle holy water while we all recited a prayer.

I half expected something extraordinary to happen, yet nothing physically occurred. We did, however, sense a presence as we moved through the rooms, accompanied by a few inexplicable noises—but nothing beyond that.

From that day forward, the matter remained private, shared only with a few close friends—until now. For about two years, the house settled, and we felt the benefit of the peace it brought.

Around that time, the activity resumed. In response, we consulted two clairvoyants to see what they might 'pick up'. The first, whom my mother had known for several years, was already aware of the problems in the house. In an unusual move, she came to our home—clients normally had to visit her—and gave my mother a reading in the dining room.

I had mentioned that, in my opinion, no one should go up to the back bedroom. Both my mother and I knew that whenever we entered, there was a feeling of something being there. The air often felt heavy, accompanied by an intuitive sense that we just wanted to get out. To my relief, the clairvoyant said it was unnecessary to go there.

She said a few things about the bedroom. First, she told my mother that whatever was there was best left alone, as any probing might only make it worse.

Then she said to empty the room, repaint it entirely in white, and hang a small Christian cross on the back wall. Leave one window slightly open, she said, lock the door, and never go back in until we moved out.

I asked whether it would be all right just to check the room, and she categorically said no. The ownership of that room was not ours. All I remember beyond this is that she made it clear a vortex had opened there, a vista to something far more sinister than we had ever experienced in the house. In short, we were to leave it well alone.

The clairvoyant's ominous pronouncement left behind a viscous silence, confirming our primal fear that the house was merely a thin veil. We were now acutely aware of the back bedroom's sinister nature, not just as a location, but as a malignant void—a chilling doorway to an unseen dimension. This malevolent presence, now clearly defined as a vortex, felt insidious, its quiet existence an existential threat that made our usual domestic worries absurd. This was no ordinary haunting; it was a looming danger, shuddering at the edges of our fragile reality.

Needless to say, we didn't decorate the room. For one thing, somebody would have had to go in there for hours, and we knew from past experience that it wouldn't be wise. Still, it was my job to go into the room from time to time to tidy it up. Since we never used it and only placed items in there occasionally, I began to realise that things were being moved about. It often took me an hour or more to tidy the bedroom.

Every time I went in there, I felt my heart beating faster and a strong sense that something was watching me. While tidying, I would often hear faint sounds from somewhere in the room and, at times, notice objects that had shifted, always just out of sight. It was always me in that back bedroom. My parents would not go in there. Ever.

As I write this now, it is easy to say that any feelings of discomfort or a sense of being watched are nothing more than paranoia. Yet most people have experienced a feeling they cannot explain — walking into a room and suddenly feeling cold, or sensing that the atmosphere somehow isn't right. Similarly, you may have met someone and immediately felt at ease with them, or, contrariwise, felt uneasy in their company for no clear reason. It was that kind of intuitive, sixth-sense feeling I experienced in that back bedroom. It simply wasn't right, and others felt the same.

About five years later, a male friend of ours, who was also a top clairvoyant — as was his wife — came to visit. During his stay, he decided to see the back bedroom.

I immediately told him about the previous clairvoyant's warning and explained that I still felt a strong presence there. I said that I believed something evil lingered in the shadows and that entering the room with the intention of communicating in any way would not be wise. He reassured me, however, that he had come into contact with all sorts of spirits and that this should be no different.

As we walked up the stairs toward the back bedroom, I saw his left shoulder move slightly backward, and he became motionless for a few seconds. Just after that, I felt something brush past me too. Well, I say brushed past — it was more of a knock to my left shoulder that made me step back, just as my clairvoyant friend had done a few stairs ahead.

There are two things I should note here. First, I felt a faint rush of air at the same moment, the kind you sense when someone passes very close to you. Second, and more worryingly at the time, whatever it was not only passed by me but also partly through my left side, leaving me shuddering and tingling with fear.

He said, 'Something just passed me on the stairway and knocked my shoulder.'

I replied, taking into account what had just happened to me as well, and said nervously, 'Look, I think it might be best if we don't bother with this. Why unsettle it?'

The air on the landing felt heavy, almost reluctant to move. Yet he carried on walking up the stairs. His footsteps seemed unnaturally loud in the silence, each one echoing as though the house were listening. Moments later he was in the back bedroom along with his wife, my parents, and me.

'Without a doubt, it's not right here,' he said quickly, glancing around as he positioned himself in the centre of the room. The air seemed colder there, the corners darker than they should have been.

'Be careful now,' said his worried wife.

I watched with a mixture of hope and dread, if that is even possible. The room had fallen utterly still. Even the faint sounds from outside seemed to stop.

Then he said, 'I am sensing a man who drowned during the Second World War.'

He began to describe the man's background, painting a clearer picture of who he was. As he spoke, a strange pressure filled the room, as though something unseen were pressing against us. It became clear that the clairvoyant was struggling. His words came out shortened and hesitant, uncharacteristic of him.

'No, stop it!' he cried.

I wondered what *it* was. The hairs on my arms were standing upright.

'Are you all right?' his now visibly shaken wife asked her increasingly anxious husband.

'He drowned, and it's making it hard for me to breathe,' he exclaimed.

Seconds later he said, 'I can't breathe,' his voice sounding moribund and grave-like. The sound of it seemed to hang in the air, flat and unnatural, as though the house itself had swallowed the words whole.

As he said this, his arms stretched out as if he were beginning to resemble a Frankenstein walking posture. The movement was stiff and unnatural, his limbs jerking as though pulled by invisible strings. Bizarrely, as his arms became fully outstretched, forming an almost perfect right angle to his body, he began to rotate his wrists in shaky, alternating semi-circles. The slow, repetitive motion made an odd whispering sound through the air.

After a few seconds of these hand movements, which were reminiscent of a magician's prestidigitation during a trick, he began to raise his hands higher. At first, I thought he could see something to touch, but it soon became clear that whatever it was lay not in front of him but within him. His hands moved closer to his throat.

The trembling ceased as his fingers found his neck, pressing tightly around it. It was not merely a gesture to show that he was struggling to breathe, but an awful,

54

physical confirmation that something was taking hold of him. His face had grown pale, and his eyes seemed to fix on something none of us could see.

In that instant, it was obvious that urgent action was needed to end the spirit communication. Then, in a strangulated, gasping voice that seemed not wholly his own, he cried out, 'I'm choking!'

The words tore through the heavy silence of the room, leaving an echo that felt heavier than sound itself.

With his final words of, 'Help me!' his wife grabbed hold of him, shouting his name as she did. He let out a huge gasp before falling slightly forward. The link with the spirit was abruptly broken. It was clearly dangerous to do, but in the circumstances, probably the lesser of two evils.

After taking a few deep breaths to restore his lungs to their normal complement of air, he looked around at us and understated what had just happened by saying, 'Hmmm, that was tough.'

Bloody frightening, I thought. The room felt heavy, as though it still held the shadow of whatever had gripped him. Even now, the silence seemed watchful, waiting for the next move.

After thanking his wife for her helpful and much-needed intercession, he said he would return the next week to explore further and try to uncover more about what was happening in the back bedroom. However, still shaken by the experience of spiritual asphyxiation, I was already halfway out of the room as he spoke. I was uneasy, having predicted that something would happen, and I could not help but wonder what might occur next if this 'Pandora's Box' of a back bedroom were opened.

I stopped walking as I heard his voice and returned to the room. I spoke my thoughts, insisting it was best left as it was. Again, my warning fell on deaf ears, sadly.

However, the clairvoyant never returned. Days before his planned visit, he fell ill, and after recovering he felt it would not be wise to explore further. Several months later, I asked him again about a possible return. His response was categorical. 'NO!'

What became clear was that the back bedroom was only the tip of the iceberg. Visiting clairvoyants, including those described earlier and later ones my mother consulted at various psychic fairs, also focused on this room. Each one told her unequivocally that it was evil and that we needed to move. We finally did so in late 1984.

Chapter Six

Deadly Heating!

Like most people, we adore central heating when it's cold outside, but for years, we were starved of good heat due to the cost. Beyond this financial pressure, our house was perpetually colder than it should have ever been. Of course, that unnatural cold was no surprise given the extent of its paranormal spookiness!

Accordingly, we welcomed the news that central heating was finally to be installed. There was a caveat, however: the council asked us to be one of the first to trial a new coal fire with a back boiler in the front room. This unit was considered an enjoyable hybrid—it offered the traditional look of a coal fire while promoting energy conservation. The boiler used the fire's heat to warm both the radiators and the domestic hot water. There were probably other reasons behind their decision to install these new heaters, but frankly, we were just delighted to have any heating at all.

To understand the peril, a few crucial details about this room heater are essential. It was a completely sealed unit, except for a small front door used for refuelling. Crucially, that door was never to be left open for long, as deadly fumes could be released, causing illness, permanent health damage, or even death.

Furthermore, the amount of coal that could be safely burnt at any one time was strictly defined as being level with the fret top and no more—a fact that would prove incredibly important. The unit was essentially a life-support system for the house: the coal fire heated a back boiler located directly behind it, which in turn warmed the radiators and the domestic hot water. While an electric immersion heater offered a summer back-up, in the winter, the fire dictated everything.

With the important details of the room heater out of the way, let me begin the story in earnest.

One night, my mother was desperately cold and made a critical mistake: she put far too much coal in the grate. Instead of keeping the coal at fret top level—the mandatory maximum—she had actually angled it upwards at 45 degrees from the fret top to the upper portion of the boiler's rear plate.

In effect, the fire's heat, which used conduction to warm the water boiler at the back, was now being well and truly maximised. When I saw this, I gently reminded her that I was sure the installer said not to bank the coal as she had done; for her, however, the prospect of warmth overrode coldness.

Over the evening, the room heater's heavy-duty metal back grew a shocking red. By 11 p.m., I was sweating with worry and knew something was seriously wrong. I opened the door and started removing the coal, piece by piece. The coal inside was glowing red, dangerously hot, and difficult to manoeuvre out of the grate and onto the hearth. My original intention was to let each piece cool down somewhat before placing it outside, as I had nowhere else safe to put it.

This painstaking process broke down within 30 minutes. I immediately resorted to just snatching the very hot coal pieces straight from the fire with tongs and rushing them to the front garden, where a second, unfortunate coal fire was now taking shape.

Halfway through this extraction, a neighbour walked by and instantly thought I'd lost it. He asked what on earth I was doing, and I quickly explained the situation. He began to laugh manically and loudly, leaning his head back to bellow his *schadenfreude* interpretation of my dilemma. But as he tilted his head upwards, looking directly over my head into the sky beyond, his laughter suddenly stopped. His face contorted, as if some great cosmic event was unfolding.

He looked back down and straight at me; I awaited some kind of cosmic revelation. The revelation came, but it was much more local. He said, with a grin that only exaggerated his amusement, 'Do you know your chimney's on fire?'

I turned around and looked up at our chimney. It was indeed on fire, with sparks and small flames emanating from it in a randomly haphazard and menacing way. I swore out loud and rushed back into the house to redouble my efforts to remove the remaining red-hot coal. My only hope was that this extraction might end the chimney fire, as well as reduce the very intense heat radiating from the room heater's heavy, solid-looking metal backplate.

In fact, on reflection, our coal fire room heater was a misnomer; it was fast becoming something akin to a kiln. Even though I had substantially removed the hot coal, the backplate continued to escalate, turning a white-hot shade of intense red. I wasn't an expert on the room heater's mechanics, but since it was a back boiler, I worried the water wasn't circulating well, preventing the heat from being drawn away as it should have been.

The backplate was slowly going white, mirroring the paleness of my own face from sheer terror. I couldn't shake the thought that the back boiler could explode. Worse still, I imagined my father arriving home from his night shift only to find his front door key was useless because the door—and the entire house—had ceased to exist!

By the time I had dangerously removed the last piece of red-hot coal, the room heater's metal back, which had only been red when I started, now glowed white-hot. Real panic set in. Was the boiler going to explode and take half the neighbourhood with it—certainly my mother and me?

At that moment, the radiators began shaking themselves apart. They were banging and rattling in a demented way, as if dancing to a rock and roll record. I ran every drop of hot water off to relieve the pressure. I have never, before or since, seen scalding water come out of a hot water tap like that; we certainly never set the thermostat that high. So much steam poured out that our bathroom looked more like a Swedish sauna within minutes.

Ten minutes later, the water temperature from the hot tap was a complete misnomer: it was not even tepid, just bone cold.

Meanwhile, the fire's backplate began to cool, showing a less menacing red colour, and, reassuringly, no white metal remained. The chimney outside, which had been spewing sparks into the night, had also settled.

And yet, within ten minutes of me running off all the extremely hot water, the radiators mysteriously performed their "rock and roll dance" again. As before, I immediately ran every single drop of hot water off, not only to stop the chaotic noise but because I was still rightly concerned about the boiler exploding. Within an hour, the back of the fire had finally cooled, and thankfully, the hot water never returned to make the radiators dance for a third time.

This heated bizarre incident was finally over. But wait, what was that noise I could hear from outside? My first thoughts were that it sounded like heavy engine noise.

Before I could figure it out, a loud knocking interrupted me at the front door. As I approached, I couldn't help but think it was a neighbour asking why a fire was still burning in the front garden. *How do you answer that?* I wondered. Volcanic fissure, perhaps!

As I opened the front door, my disbelief about the evening's events took a step into the completely surreal. Seized by a Victor Meldrew urge, I suppressed the desire to shriek loudly, 'I don't believe it!'

Standing before me was a fireman, and behind him, parked on the road, was a full-sized fire engine with multiple flashing blue lights. Additionally, a gathering audience of neighbours stood outside by our gate and front garden hedge, all watching to see what the fuss was about. I had no idea myself. Standing right behind me in the hallway, my mother's demeanour—composed yet utterly disbelieving—was no help at all.

'Evening, Sir. We've received a call that your chimney's on fire!' the palpably concerned fireman stated.

'Yes, I'm afraid it was, but it's out now,' I replied, deeply embarrassed, hoping my tone would convey that I just wanted the entire surreal ordeal to end.

'Best get your chimney cleaned as soon as possible!' he insisted.

'It was, a few weeks back!' I quickly retorted.

'That's odd,' he said, his expression one of growing disbelief that perfectly matched our own. 'Perhaps call them back, just to make sure.'

'Yes, sure, will do!' I promised.

He then looked at me quizzically, as if wondering whether I would actually fulfil this promise.

His attention was briefly diverted. He glanced over his right shoulder, then looked back at me, ready to ask the question I think the entire ensemble gathered by our front garden hedge and gate wanted answered:

'Are you aware you've got a domestic coal fire currently burning in your front garden?'

'Yes, my mother told me to put it out!' I replied, completely missing the sardonic irony of the statement.

'Best put that out with some water, then,' he advised, giving me a perplexed look—one that mirrored my neighbour's from earlier.

As the fireman turned to walk away, there in the background, standing outside by the front gate, was that very neighbour. He was clearly absorbing the second and final part of my evening's entertainment. He gave me a knowing smile, and then began to walk back to his house.

As he walked away, the neighbour shouted back over his shoulder, 'You ought to write a book about your house, Colin!'

'One day,' I muttered softly in his direction, 'it will happen—one day.'

The emergency services were gone as quickly as they arrived, putting a strange end to a bizarre evening. Yet, the incident wasn't purely a mechanical failure. Three specific points about that night, in particular, suggested the paranormal was involved.

First, the following morning, the plumber confirmed my original thought: the water circulation had indeed become blocked. Without that flow, the heat couldn't be removed by the water, and so it got hotter and hotter inside the boiler, hence the shocking redness of the fire's back. However, it was inexplicable why the boiler didn't explode or completely melt down, given the immense heat and non-circulation of water.

Secondly, there was the matter of the water itself: how it became so scalding (the steam from the hot tap was unbelievable), and then, crucially, how it reheated in just ten minutes. The plumber told me, without equivocation, that such a rapid reheating could not take place in such a short time, even if the immersion heater had been on, which it wasn't.

When I insisted that it did happen that quickly, and my mother confirmed it, he simply looked at us, shrugged his shoulders while laughing, and said, 'That's weird and not possible.' Without any further addition, he just perfunctorily left.

Third, as the room heater had been removed, we took the opportunity to get the chimney inspected and fully swept. We asked the chimney sweep to specifically check for residual soot that might have been the source of the flames and sparks.

On inspection, he found nothing in the lower half of the chimney that would suggest a fire had even taken place, or higher up, even in the stack itself. Very little soot was removed this time around. He told my mother that the flames and sparks she reported were absolutely not a result of any remaining soot inside the chimney. He went on to say that as only dirty, sooty chimneys caught fire, and ours was the complete opposite, he was at a loss to explain why ours did.

No rational explanation could be found for the chimney fire, and there was no external damage to the roof either. In effect, since there was no residual evidence to suggest a chimney fire ever occurred, it was left to us to support each other that it did. Thank God the neighbour saw it, otherwise we all would have been convinced we'd suffered from a vivid, collective delusion!

I'd just like to add a final note regarding the neighbour. His advice wasn't casual; having witnessed the multitude of strange and paranormal happenings in our house, he knew people simply wouldn't believe our accounts. His suggestion to write a book was spoken in 1981. Thirty-eight years later, in 2019, I finally honoured his prediction and put pen to paper, as it were.

Another room heater we had somehow inexplicably developed a split in the chimney flue, leaking carbon monoxide into the front room where we sat most evenings. For months, we had grown increasingly tired and sick without explanation, our alertness deteriorating the more we used the fire. By the end, had we not discovered the leak by accident, the outcome would have been fatal: we would have simply fallen asleep and never woken up.

If we thought installing a new gas fire would solve our problems, we were wrong.

We were told it would take just one day to remove the old fire and replace it with a new gas one. The plumber duly arrived and began the job. Yes, I said *plumber* — though he assured me he'd been retrained to fit gas fires after a one-day course. Something about the situation didn't feel right. Maybe it was the sparks flying off the concrete near the gas pipe that made me uneasy. When I asked if he knew what he was doing, he just laughed and said everything was under control.

As it turned out, the job stretched into a second day. The new fire was left half-installed overnight, awaiting completion the following morning. Before going to bed, I decided to check that the front room windows were locked — and to see the mess the *gas fitter* had left behind. I didn't expect to find anything wrong, but as the idiom goes, *better safe than sorry*. He had assured me before leaving that everything was shut off and safe.

As soon as I opened the front room door, I was hit by the heavy, intoxicating smell of gas. Surely not! My first instinct was to switch on the light — but I had a sudden moment of clarity. That would have been a *very* bad idea. Instead, I opened all the windows, then the front door, trying not to panic.

I called my mother from the kitchen, and when she came in, she couldn't believe it either. She immediately panicked and told me to fetch our neighbour — the one who was good with household repairs — to see if he could confirm the leak.

A few minutes later, he appeared in the doorway... smoking a cigarette.

I couldn't believe my eyes. For a few terrifying seconds he just stood there, casually puffing away, until I managed to stammer that gas and an open flame were a deadly combination. He swore, realizing what he'd done, and ran outside to stub it out.

When he returned, he took a few cautious sniffs, then laughed.

'Definitely a leak,' he said. 'I could smell it as I passed by your front room windows.' We both examined the half-installed gas fire, trying to find the source, but we couldn't pinpoint it. So I called the out-of-hours gas emergency line. Thirty minutes later, the engineer arrived, tested the supply pipe, and found a small leak.

He explained that if we'd gone to bed as planned, the gas would have built up overnight and exploded the moment someone turned on a light switch — likely when they came down in the morning, smelled gas, and flicked the switch. *Boom.*

I told the gas engineer about the neighbour entering the room smoking a cigarette, and he simply said, 'You were lucky!' More so as the room was ventilated by the chimney, only emphasising how bad the leak was.

It wasn't the only near-miss we ever had, but it's the one that still makes my heart race whenever I think about it.

Years earlier, in our old house, the rising gas main pipe leading into the meter had been severely dented—at least 50% constriction—right from the day it was installed. I complained at the time, but was told it was fine. I even recall one engineer coming out. Before he had even touched or examined the pipe, he laughed and said the callout was 'hilarious,' insisting, 'It's all right. Nothing to worry about.'

Nevertheless, I kept checking that cupboard, cleaning it, straightening it. The rest of the family simply threw things in without a thought. I didn't understand the technicalities of gas flow in a pipe—*Increased Pressure Upstream* and *Turbulent Flow and Vibration*—but I knew something wasn't right, it just seemed profoundly hazardous. I asked people who emptied the gas meter if they thought it was abnormal; it received varying opinions, but all agreed they had never seen a dent like that before.

66

When the system was finally replaced in the 1970s, it wasn't just that single pipe that was removed. All the gas pipes—from outside, through the house, and into the meter—were stripped out and replaced.

Before installation, when a senior gas engineer saw the dent, he gasped in amazement—then, incredulously, initially blamed us for causing it. He repeated it a second time, laughing lightly, as if I were trying to banjax him with some untruth. I hastily explained it had been like that from day one, and we had been told it was all right. He then became even more shocked. The engineer said the system could have easily escalated to being potentially life-threatening and was astonished it had never been dealt with sooner.

Looking back, it's clear that whatever force had been at work in that house kept us alive, yet never removed the danger entirely. We teetered on the edge more times than I can count—close enough to disaster that it was impossible to ignore. Somehow, in ways that defy logic, we were both endangered and preserved, played off between danger and safety, between sanity and the sense of being pushed over the precipice, leaving behind an unsettling contradiction between the logical world and our surreal experiences.

Chapter Seven

Don't Let The Bed Ghost Bite!

Are you sitting—or perhaps even lying—comfortably? I ask because this chapter involves the absolute vulnerability of lying in bed. The moment when we are suspended between wakefulness and sleep, the precise moment when the paranormal may come a calling. Think about it: when you are in bed, you drop your conscious guard, relaxing and settling in, seeking respite. At that point, you are at your most defenceless.

Most people do not like the dark. Not because it necessarily harbours something malevolent, but because in darkness, shadows may twist and flicker, and every familiar shapes may warp, as if the room itself is changing, moving ever so slightly.

After I moved into the small front bedroom, my brother was left to sleep alone in the dreaded back bedroom. It was late one night when I was wrenched abruptly from sleep. I looked up to see him standing by my bed, utterly consumed by fear. He wasn't just shaking; he was practically vibrating, a tremor that ran right up from his voice.

'Colin,' he whispered, his voice a tight, high cord of sheer anxiety.

'What?' I mumbled, still wrestling with the heavy, confusing haze of sleep.

'There's someone in my room,' he repeated, the worry now sharp and unmistakable.

68

'Huh!' That was all I could manage, waiting for him to explain, certain he had to be imagining things.

'There is someone walking around my room, and I am terrified. Please, come and help me,' he pleaded—a reply I never expected.

I must say my brother was the sturdier of the two of us, the tougher, the one who rarely faltered. He carried more bravado and, being five years my senior, more authority. Yet here he was, battle-weary from the room itself, his voice tight with fear, asking for my help in a way he never had before. A chill ran through me. Although I trusted his judgement implicitly, I still felt uneasy about going in there.

Suddenly he kneeled down and looked me in the face, trying to enforce his request. He was pleading with me to go with him, scared—scared like I had never seen him before. Petrified would be a better word. Reluctantly, I got up and followed him towards his darkened bedroom. He stopped just inside the doorway and looked back at me, eyes wide, as if a firing squad—or something far worse—waited silently in the gloom.

'Go on!' I whispered softly. At my quiet urging, he immediately turned and slipped back into his bedroom.

He climbed into the left side of his bed, and I walked around to the right. Even at eight or nine, I felt an instant unease about the situation. My goal was simple: if I could calm my brother's fears about footsteps around his bed, we would both sleep more easily in our separate rooms later.

Just picture this: it's about 2 a.m. Two brothers nervously grip the top sheet and duvet in the dark, listening and trying to sense something that is not "existential," at least not in the strict, empirical scientific sense. One brother is terrified—

69

my elder brother—while the other wrestles with ghostly cognitive polemics. The only things visible in the bed are our heads above the sheet and two sets of hands, clutching the covers in anxious anticipation of a close encounter with *The Unknown*—the paranormal kind.

'Well, can you hear or feel footsteps?' he asked before I had a chance to sense anything.

'Not yet. Let me lie here and see what I can feel,' I replied, irritation creeping into my voice.

Just moments later… 'There! There it is!' he exclaimed, excitement and fear mingling in his tone.

'What?' I asked. I didn't know what to say. I was torn between listening, feeling for paranormal vibrations, worrying about the situation, and absorbing my brother's palpable anxiety. The combination left me cognitively immobilised.

'Footsteps around the bed! Can't you feel it?' he pressed, as if I wouldn't have reported it if I truly felt it myself.

Lying there, my brother's words went cold—and so did the room. I began to feel insecure about what was happening outside the bed. I wanted to pull the covers up and over me to blot out everything. Without warning, I felt footsteps around the bed, just as if somebody was really there. I thought, no way was this happening, surely! The sheets began to be pulled downwards and somebody sat on the edge of the bed, causing it to bend down on the left corner, my brother's side of the bed.

That was it for my brother. He jumped out and ran onto the landing. 'I'm sure he said 'get out.' I stayed in the bed, bravado more than brains, I think. But I soon succumbed, though not by running out, as my brother had. I tried to act cool and detached, getting up slowly and walking back round the bed to the door. As I passed along the bottom left side, I was both scared and astonished to see the corner of the bed pushed down, just as if something were sitting there or pressing down on it.

'I'm not going back in there tonight,' he remonstrated softly but firmly.

Chills ran down my spine as he asked, eerily, 'Did you feel footsteps?' I replied ominously in the affirmative.

My poor brother was thoroughly spooked and had every right to be. After his first suggestion—to sleep on my bedroom floor—was politely, if regretfully, declined, he ended up sleeping downstairs on the sofa. That morning, we told our mother and once again resolved to follow through with the plans to move we had discussed so many times before.

Months later, my brother was still experiencing unsettling events in the back bedroom, yet he had grown to accept them, even managing to sleep through the disturbances. Brave, brave man. I, however, was far less composed. When the same thing happened to me, it was worse.

The disturbance began with something sitting on my bed, the sheets tugged forcefully, but the worst was the sensation of a finger slowly tracing up my left leg to my knees, or along my left arm. It never stopped, even when I kicked out and foolishly shouted, 'Stop it!'

Remarkably, it was always my left side. Why this side? The paranormal respects no physical boundaries, so the repetition was inexplicable. This intrusive contact often preceded or followed a horrifying addition: the sound of a presence breathing near me. When I felt the finger tracing

71

my skin and then heard a deep exhale, my trepidation went off the scale, triggering every expected physical reaction of someone sensing a threat.

Looking back, these experiences illustrate how naked darkness, capable of subjugating rational senses, can magnify fear and temporarily suffocate our grasp on reality. In such moments, our mortal fragility—and vulnerability to all things that go bump in the night—is laid bare.

Occasionally, something would kick the end of the bed. Some were more than mere kicks; I could feel the bed rock or shake briefly. What made most of these kicks especially eerie was their muffled quality. Imagine a trumpet player using a mute to soften the sound—that was exactly how these kicks felt: deliberately muted, yet unnervingly precise.

My mother also reported similar events: something sitting on her side of the bed, the bottom of the bed being kicked, usually within the first twenty minutes of getting in. As with my brother, we gradually became battle-hardened. I suspect most others would not have had such resilience. They would have fled.

Chapter Eight

Spectrum of Manifestations

The following chapter contains fourteen short anecdotes recounting various encounters with *The Unknown*. These are the only ones of this brevity I can recall; over the course of several decades, others have inevitably faded, now lost to memory.

The Back Bedroom

It's fair to say that if something flew through the air, you'd be the first one out the door — for good. And who could blame you? Ghostly goings-on are best left to films and folklore, not the front room. Yet for years, our house was alive with things that refused explanation: footsteps where no one walked, a chill in the air that came from nowhere, fleeting shadows at the corner of your vision.

To anyone living a 'normal' life, it would've been all wrong. Most people would've been off down the road shouting, 'Hasta la vista, baby!' And truthfully, that's how it should have been for us too.

When my parents moved into the house in 1952, my mother quickly sensed that it was, as she put it, *active*. She had been psychic for as long as I could remember — not in the theatrical way, but quietly, as if she could hear a frequency the rest of us missed. She died at seventy-six, never realising her true potential, living a modest life in service of her husband.

Though the entire house had its moments, the back bedroom, hallway, and stairs were always the worst — our so-called *hotspots*. The back bedroom in particular carried a weight about it, as though the air itself resisted being breathed.

The first real sign that something was wrong came when my newly married uncle and aunt stayed there after their wedding. They were meant to be with us for a few weeks while waiting for their council house. As it turned out, they didn't last nearly that long.

I only learned what happened years later. One evening, decades after the fact, we were talking about the strange atmosphere in that room when my uncle quietly said, 'You know, I stayed in there once.'

Until then, he hadn't believed in anything psychic or ghostly — quite the opposite. But as he began to tell me what happened, even thirty years later, the memory still gripped him. His hands shook slightly as he spoke, and though he smiled now and then, I could tell a chill was creeping up his spine. After all, he was sitting in the very house where it had all happened.

The first incident came one early morning. He woke abruptly to see two figures standing at the end of the bed. They were still at first — human-shaped but not quite solid, faintly glowing, their outlines rippling as if underwater. Before he could move, they began to drift closer.

Panic seized him. In one motion, he shoved his wife off the bed toward the door, barking at her to get out. He hauled himself across the mattress using the sheets for leverage —

his version of an emergency escape. She shouted in confusion, and he shouted back, but neither could drown out the cold dread filling the room. Even as he scrambled after her, the figures still stood there, closing in.

He said he'd never known fear like it. For months afterwards, he avoided that room entirely. His wife later confirmed she'd seen the same thing.

The second episode happened not long after. Once again, he woke early — this time to find the curtains completely ablaze. Flames licked upward toward the ceiling, orange light pulsing across the walls. The heat, the roar — it all seemed so real he could smell it. Without thinking, he pushed his poor wife off the bed again and bolted onto the landing with her. But when they looked back, there was nothing. No smoke, no scorch marks. Only darkness.

That was enough. They packed their things and left soon after.

When he finished telling me all this, I asked if he thought he might have dreamed it. He shook his head with quiet certainty.

'No,' he said.

I asked if anything else had ever happened. He gave a weary smile and replied, 'Wasn't that enough?'

∞

Spirit Fights

Between the ages of six and sixteen, about once a month during dream sleep, I would be involved in a 'spirit fight' with what seemed to be the same malevolent entity.

75

It appeared to take delight in tussling and fighting with me. Often, I would end up being thrown around my bedroom, hitting the walls hard. Although the pain was slight, I remember a feeling akin to being winded.

This entity would push me up against the walls, and in response, I would try to fight it—quite how, I'm not sure. I just felt as if I were trying to force it away mentally, and at times, with my arms. I remember the sensation of my arms being pushed or clamped against my sides as I was forced upwards against a wall.

On other occasions, I felt a hand against my throat, causing the same upward movement. It always seemed, for the most part, to be the same room in my dreams—my bedroom. I say seemed because I don't really remember the furniture, only what felt like the walls of my bedroom.

However, although the same room appeared in all of these dreams, this struggle wasn't confined to my bedroom but also took place in what seemed to be another room next door. I often recall moving through the walls as if they weren't physically there.

The struggle was, in many ways, violent—an unmistakable attack on me. I sometimes managed to fight back and remember pushing this force away, seemingly hurting it at times. When that happened, I felt better, even laughed, and occasionally went towards it—a bad idea. I always seemed to receive far more 'hurt' than I ever gave… or even tried to.

Most times, when I awoke from these dreams, I experienced a rush of adrenaline and a feeling of exhaustion, as if I had been in a real physical altercation. I felt shaken, with mild body pain and a temporary sense of cognitive disorientation. Such dreams occurred irregularly during those years. Overall, I suppose I had them about once a month in that house during the period mentioned above. Each was similar in setting and duration, though some seemed to last longer.

Given all the other strange things that happened in the house at that time, I saw these sleep events as yet another aberration of the house's activity. I cannot remember ever telling anyone about them, even though, as you can imagine, they were distressing, exhausting, and mentally draining.

Such events suggested I was under *psychic attack* from something that, I believe, also manifested elsewhere in the house. I'm sure some would say these dreams reflected an inner conflict—me fighting myself. Well, that sounds plausible enough, but unlikely.

∞

Tugged, Shoved, And Scared

Manifestations took varying forms — from appearances to bodily contact, and everything in between. I will now run through a cornucopia of things that, while separate, are clearly connected.

Areas where *things* happened quite regularly were the stairway and hallway. By this, I mean it was not unusual to feel that *eyes* were upon you, or to experience a deep sense of unease when walking through the hallway or using the stairs; it was often colder there than it should have been. My mother and I seemed to be the main recipients of this unusual activity. Often, as we used the stairway, we were *knocked* by something, as though someone were brushing past us in the opposite direction. On a couple of occasions, I remember being pushed down the stairs and grabbing the banister rail to prevent a dangerous fall. As you can imagine, this was deeply disturbing, and even now, as I write about it, I still feel a chill inside.

Once, after getting out of the bath and wrapping a towel around my waist, it was tugged twice, firmly, as if something were trying to pull it down. Another time, a tightly wrapped towel was undone before my eyes and pulled away onto the floor. I ran out of the bathroom naked, clutching another towel to preserve my modesty. My mother told me that on several occasions over the years, similar towel-pulling incidents had happened to her as well.

On another occasion, my mother reported something quite extraordinary while sitting on the toilet with the door open. As she sat there, something began to form outside on the landing. She said the apparition first appeared at the feet, then slowly continued upwards, revealing both legs at the same time — almost as if a sheet were being raised gradually to uncover someone. When it reached the knees, the forming paused briefly before continuing upward. By the time it had reached halfway up the thighs — perhaps thirty seconds after it began — my mother slammed the toilet door shut.

She said it was a man, judging by the clothes, but beyond that she never elaborated. Still, quite remarkable, wouldn't you agree? I used to tease her about it sometimes, saying she should have waited to see what happened next. She always replied, 'I was on the toilet!'

∞

Seen And Heard, Yet Never There

However, what we saw through the kitchen windows, or from the dining room that connected to the kitchen, were apparitions. For about a decade, ghostly figures haunted us. They walked past our kitchen windows and around the corner of the house to the back door. By both sight and sound, it was unmistakably clear that these visitors were real—at least to us.

Our side path—along with the neighbour's adjacent path—was simply a straight line of rectangular paving stones, with no gravel or chippings anywhere. Normally, walking along it produced only dull, muffled footsteps. Yet countless times, we heard someone approaching with the sharp crunch of heavy boots on gravel or chippings.

My mother and I could hear it distinctly. The sound would grow louder and louder, as if the person were walking along a path at least ten or fifteen yards long. Eventually, as the footsteps reached the window, a man would appear. He had dark hair, a face suggesting he was in his early to late twenties, sharp features, and noticeable sideburns. This man appeared several times over the years.

Naturally, I would rush to the back door, expecting to see someone. Each time, consternation gripped me when there was nothing there. It was deeply unnerving. I remember glimpsing one or two other figures, though their details escape me now. Yet every time I opened the back door, no one was there.

On one occasion, even my father saw someone. How did he react? He was clearly unnerved and unsettled, taking days to come to terms with what he had witnessed. Yet, despite

79

hearing about these apparitional events many times, and understanding their cumulative effect on our nerves, it still didn't prompt him to take any action toward moving house.

I should add at this juncture that I never believed his particular mindset about our desired house move was born of indifference toward us. It was more a lack of understanding, no doubt resulting from: (a) his night work, which created emotional distance from our everyday lives and experiences; and (b) his duties outside of work, which encompassed several areas and, in totality, pulled him away from the house both physically and emotionally.

Anyway, back to these apparitions!

I remember how we often heard a woman's high heels clicking along our path, growing louder and louder, heralding her impending passage past our windows. And indeed, she appeared.

My mother and I both saw the same thing: a side profile of a woman's head with an incredible beehive hairstyle—a beehive of real class! She looked attractive, blonde-haired, and about thirty years old from her profile. Like the man described earlier, we saw this woman several times over the years. On one occasion, when I heard the footsteps and saw her close up through the kitchen windows, I ran to the back door to see her—but, as usual, no one was there.

There were only two occasions when our neighbour happened to be outside her back door—which overlooked both our kitchen windows and back door—and could potentially confirm or deny what we had seen. The first time, she was putting rubbish in her bin; on the other, she was simply standing outside her own back door. On both occasions, I asked if she had seen or heard anyone walk up our side path, past our kitchen windows, and round to our back door. She looked at me as if I were certifiable. Of course, unless she had seen what we saw, her reaction was entirely understandable.

∞

Auditory Activity

On many occasions, over several years—or perhaps even longer—we would hear the front door being closed loudly. At times, this was accompanied by the sound of a bicycle being pushed along the hallway and left where my mother would occasionally place it. I cannot recall the number of times I heard the door slam and, expecting my mother—who was due home—to be there, walked to the hallway, only to find that she never entered.

Even when my mother was already home, and we heard the front door close loudly (followed by the bicycle sounds), I would still go to the hallway out of curiosity. As you can imagine, this became both confusing and frustrating, especially since even the next-door neighbours reported hearing the door slam. Over the years, it grew increasingly unnerving, adding yet another layer to the many other paranormal experiences we had witnessed. All in all, it was just very, very strange.

∞

Return Of The Cat

Once there was a beautiful mottled cat that frequented our front garden. Its owners, who lived several houses down the road, had thrown it out, and it took refuge under a hedge near our front door.

The problem was twofold: the weather was growing cold, and we had a dog who seriously did not like cats. Whenever we let him out the front, he would head straight for the cat with such unerring accuracy it would make a Tomahawk missile blush. To avoid trouble, we limited his visits to the back garden, but even that soon became problematic. I discovered who the owners were and asked if they would take it back. They agreed, and I returned it—but within days, the cat was back under our hedge. I asked again, but this time it was a firm 'no'.

At least once a day, the cat would jump onto the front room window ledge. Its narrow landing caused it to bump against the windows, announcing its presence inside. It meowed incessantly for attention, and I would either speak to it through the window or go outside to stroke it, which it adored.

Often, I had to tell it to go because our dog would go berserk barking. We longed to keep it, but being unable to do so made its persistent meowing—especially in the cold— nearly unbearable. If I acknowledged it through the window, I could usually coax it to jump down. Soon, it became clear that the cat was disturbing neighbours and their dogs, who reacted as most dogs do when confronted by a surprise feline. It was also growing more feral, sometimes reacting aggressively to humans.

Efforts to rehome it—through the RSPCA, its owners, and other means—proved fruitless. Eventually, as the cat became more reactive to harsh outdoor conditions, our dog's behaviour, and passing strangers, I learned it had been put down.

And here is where the story takes a truly eerie turn. After it was put down, it returned. For weeks, we would hear it jump onto the window ledge—the same bumps, the same meows. Sometimes I ran to the window to see it, but it was never there. I went outside; still nothing. The sounds were so vivid, so exact, that they seemed alive. After several weeks of pleading with it to go, speaking through the window to what was obviously nothing, it finally stopped.

To this day, this event saddens me, but it also makes me wonder about the spirits of animals. Spiritualists often say that, just as humans pass into the next life, animals do too. We are, in effect, reunited with our loved ones—human and animal alike. Perhaps one day science will acknowledge dimensions beyond our own, where the familiar laws of physics no longer apply. Perhaps this was one such glimpse.

∞

A Chair On The Table, The Sleeping Boy

More generally, countless other strange things happened, though some have probably been forgotten forever. A few, however, can be recounted here. Their brevity should not diminish their significance; these were simply short, unsettling episodes.

One morning, I went downstairs and entered the dining room to find my mother looking at me with a perplexed expression. She asked why I had placed one of the dining room chairs on the table—something we never did. Of course, I hadn't done it. It was shrugged off as yet another bizarre incident.

On several occasions, I witnessed objects appear or disappear before my eyes, such as coins. Lights would flicker inexplicably. Strange smells—like bad eggs, or even sulphur—would sometimes drift through the house.

One night, as I was heading to bed, I noticed my parents' bedroom door was ajar. The small opening allowed a sliver of light to illuminate part of their room. As I passed by, the illumination seemed particularly focused on my father's side of the bed. Yet, I didn't see my father there. Instead, a child, about nine or ten years old, lay in his place.

Disbelieving my eyes, I entered the room very quietly, keeping my gaze fixed on the child. I could see him clearly, noting his facial features and short dark hair. I walked around the bed to my father's side, and the boy remained there, fast asleep, facing toward my mother.

The following morning, I told my mother what I had seen. To my surprise, she said she had woken several times over the years and seen this same boy, exactly as I had described him.

∞

Battery Drainage

When I was young, I had a cassette recorder. I had to buy batteries for it because the charger was prohibitively expensive as a one-off purchase. I needed good-quality batteries, too, because the cheaper ones never lasted long, and even the more expensive ones seemed to run out far sooner than they should.

I remember many times I opened new packs of four well-known branded batteries and, within just thirty minutes, they were completely drained. They should have lasted for hours. This unusual-battery drainage puzzled everyone I asked about it. Even the shop retailers where I bought the batteries seemed to think, quite incorrectly, that I was playing some trick on them.

It didn't take long for me to realise that this unexplainable, rapid battery drainage was a telltale sign of an active house.

∞

Moving Objects

On countless occasions, objects moved with a clear, unsettling purpose—sometimes a subtle shift at the corner of our eyes, and other times a direct displacement that left no room for doubt. My mother's large collection of ornaments provided an endless supply of targets, constantly reminding us that the house's pervasive paranormal activity was present in every single room.

∞

Walnut Wardrobe Scratches, Back Bedroom Tidying

In the late 1970s, my parents purchased a beautiful two-piece walnut wardrobe set from family neighbours. It was immaculate and simply stunning to look at. Over the course of four years, my father accidentally splashed aftershave on it, leaving some whitish, patchy marks. Aside from that, however, the wardrobe remained in excellent condition, retaining its overall beauty. Around 1981, the set was moved into the back bedroom to make way for a new bedroom set, three years before we eventually sold it when we moved.

What was truly strange, however, was that over time, scratch marks appeared on the front of the smaller wardrobe. I do not recall if the larger one had any, as I only noticed the scratches while occasionally tidying the room. Astonished, I asked my mother to take a look.

After some initial protest, she claimed she didn't want to enter the back bedroom but agreed to come in briefly with me, we walked over to the smaller wardrobe. I pointed out the scratches, though they were obvious enough. She looked at them, shrugged, and left. By then, nothing seemed unusual to her; in fact, she later admitted that just being in the room felt torturous, judging by her expressions.

The scratches themselves resembled those made by a nail, similar to what one might use in wood or walls, run vertically along the walnut. They were fine scratches, numbering around twenty, with varying depths. None, as I recall, were particularly deep, though you could feel them if you ran your finger over them. Their lengths varied from a few inches to several, with most being fairly long.

Since I was the only one to enter the back bedroom, and even then very infrequently, how these multiple, long scratches appeared remains a mystery; a distinctly spooky one. Adding to the strangeness, the natural walnut grain on the wardrobe doors created beautiful lines from top to bottom. On certain occasions, the scratches seemed to align with these patterns, producing curious, almost deliberate formations.

Of itself, the scratches were not unusual. What made the situation truly spooky, however, was that over the few years the wardrobes remained in the back bedroom, two grotesque, almost gargoyle-like faces appeared (one on each door), roughly symmetrical in position. Each face measured about two to three inches in length and around two inches in width.

I tried to banish any thoughts of them, but they were undeniably there. This was no case of pareidolia: the tendency to perceive a familiar image or pattern where none actually exists.

When I pointed them out to my mother, she immediately saw them and exclaimed, 'I didn't need to do it!' Then, recoiling in horror, she walked straight out of the room.

The faces had not been present when my parents originally bought the wardrobes; at that time, I used to admire the simple linear patterns of the wood, which were far less complicated. Whatever had somehow formed on the doors was certainly not apotropaic, something intended to ward off evil or bad luck. Intriguingly, the emergence of these two sinister faces coincided exactly with the appearance of the multiple scratches.

Moving furniture around the back bedroom, pausing to have a cup of tea, and then returning only to question whether you had actually placed something where it was felt certainly unnerving. Out-of-sight movement of objects was infrequent, but it did occur.

On one occasion, while tidying, I made a cup of tea to take a short break. As I sat, I heard movement upstairs. I was the only one in the house at the time. My initial reaction was to rush up, but I tried to appear calm, even though I was anything but. Several minutes later, when I entered the room, I noticed minor adjustments to some objects.

Experiences like this were common whenever I tidied the back bedroom. I simply ignored them and finished the job, as the discomfort of being in that space was ever-present. Tidying the room should never have been required—it wasn't used—but like all things, I just got on with it.

∞

House Spectres

Both my mother and I would tell each other about seeing people looking out of our windows as we approached the house. My first such experience occurred when I was walking up a hill to the house after school. From a distance of about 40 to 50 yards, I could clearly see the front room windows. To the inside right of the windows stood an older woman with grey hair, looking out; I didn't recognise her, but assumed she might be a visitor.

I watched her for a few seconds, and then she was gone. I cannot recall whether she moved while I looked or simply vanished when I looked away briefly.

Entering the house, I was thoroughly spooked. I searched from room to room, only to discover that there was no one there—and had not been for several hours. Chilling, especially for a boy of seven!

Inside the house, the experiences were no less strange. Whether sitting in the front room watching television or walking through the house, we often saw shapes and ghostly, cloudy forms seemingly disappear through walls. On occasions when my mother and I both witnessed the same phenomenon, we could confirm what the other saw, and felt genuinely amazed. Sometimes we joked that we had taken them by surprise by looking or walking their way! Though, of course, that was very unlikely.

$$\infty$$

The Back Bedroom Window

Evidently, over the years, the house shaped our family in ways that are better understood qualitatively than quantitatively. In this qualitative sense, its influence was profound. So many experiences occurred that the smaller ones have faded with time, as noted earlier. When recalling events, memories often bounce off one another, bringing to life moments once forgotten. This is one of those times of reflection.

Although I cannot recall my earliest years, I must have slept in the back bedroom as well. My first memories likely begin around age five, so the experience that follows probably happened between five and seven. The bedroom always felt heavy, a place you would avoid if anywhere else was available. Yet my brother and I slept there nonetheless.

One experience I had was an inexplicable, recurring urge, almost a compulsion, to jump out of the back bedroom window. Why? It was as silly then as it is to recall now. Yet the desire was so strong that I remember, on several occasions, climbing onto the ledge, legs dangling fifteen feet above the ground, holding tightly to the window frame. Frightened, I later told my mother about this strange impulse. Had I jumped, the jagged, uneven concrete pavement, gutter, and path below would have broken my fall.

Sitting there, it felt as if some external force was trying to push me: *Go on, jump*. At the same time, another feeling warned, *Don't do it—you'll get hurt*. These opposing feelings seemed almost like separate entities: one malign, one protective. At one point, I nearly let go—but something pulled me back.

Writing this today still sends a chill down my spine. The possibility that, at such a young age, I might have been influenced by something in that back bedroom is unsettling.

Once my parents moved me to the smaller front bedroom, the thoughts vanished. At the time, I was both surprised and worried that such an urge had occurred. My mother, overburdened by the pressures of raising a family and working, had little time to address it fully—but her care likely prevented something worse.

Fortunately, I never jumped. Yet every time I returned to that back bedroom years later to tidy, I would glance at the window and remember the days when I had almost—just almost—ended my life abruptly. It was as embarrassing to recall as it was stupid in its objective.

$$\infty$$

The Uninvited Expression

My mother always had a sixth sense. She saw things others didn't—sometimes even the same things I saw.

One afternoon, I was at the window in my parents' bedroom, looking down toward the front gate. The sun was low, the light metallic and sharp, slicing the garden in half. My mother was just returning home. She stopped at the gate, her hand on the latch, and looked up at me.

Her stare lingered too long. It was fixed—intent, as if she were peering past me, through me. A flicker of surprise passed over her face, then something slower, stranger—a dawning recognition that made my stomach tighten.

Time seemed to stretch. I could feel the air thicken. The faint rustle of leaves sounded impossibly loud, and a cold prickle ran across my skin.

When she finally came inside, I met her in the hallway.

'What was that?' I asked. 'You looked like you'd seen a ghost.'

She didn't answer immediately. Then she said, softly,

'As I looked up at you, your face changed. It was my mother's face, just for a second. She was smiling at me.' I froze, the words hanging like ice in the air.

'How clearly could you see her?

'As clearly as I see you now,' she said.

Her tone left no doubt—she had seen her. Not a trick of the light, not a memory, but a visitation.

It had never happened before, and it never happened again.

I hadn't much liked her mother, and that added a strange weight to the moment. For an instant, as my mother stared up from the gate, I felt something brush across my face—not the wind, not my imagination—but as if another expression had pressed itself into mine, fleeting and impossible.

My mother could see I was shaken. She added,

'Don't worry. She wouldn't harm you in any way. She was just trying to say hello to me. I'm sure it won't happen again.'

I didn't question it. What disturbed me wasn't what I'd experienced, but that something so profound could do that, step through me, unbidden, as if my body were a metaphysical conduit. I had encountered the paranormal before, but this was different: it claimed me from within, however briefly. It was uninvited, and that alone made it unsettling.

$$\infty$$

The Sound Of Breathing

Over the years, I occasionally heard unexplained sounds. Some may have been natural, but one persisted almost constantly: breathing. Sometimes it was a single, deep exhalation; on rarer occasions, actual inhalation and exhalation could be heard, intermittently, even for several minutes. The deep exhalation suggested something voluminous or powerful, perhaps both.

I remember one occasion clearly: I was reading a book in my bedroom when the exhalation sounded as if it were only a few feet away. Frozen with fear, I gripped my book, uncertain of what might happen next. My mother, too, sometimes heard it, though she could never explain it. On the rarer occasions when full breathing was heard, its sound was both muffled and distant, yet somehow close, an impossible proximity that made it all the more unnerving.

Whether partial or full, the breathing played havoc with our senses, implying the presence of someone—or something—when, visually, there was nothing at all.

∞

Review

All of these short anecdotes, from the deepest exhalation to fleeting spectres, from the sounds and sights of things that weren't there to objects being tugged or moved, bore the same chilling signature. Each occurrence, to a greater or lesser degree, was profoundly unnerving, unequivocally spooky, and undeniably paranormal.

Chapter Nine

Twenty Yards Of Perpetual Despair

Can you imagine living in a house like this? I should also mention doors that closed slowly, without any apparent force; light shades that moved for no reason; and the unnerving sensation of someone standing directly behind, or even slightly above, you, making your nerves feel as if your very essence were under threat.

Then there were the endless problems with electrical products. A new hi-fi unit, bought by my parents as a Christmas present, burned out not once, but twice in the months following purchase. Even a friend who repaired such equipment for a living eventually scratched his head in bewilderment, unable to explain why it had happened.

Moreover, when the hi-fi unit was returned to the manufacturer's technical department, exhaustive analysis could not explain the faults—they even blamed me for causing them! I should also mention the 'bumps in the night', the constant feeling of being drained while in the house, and the relief of feeling better when away. Family members often refused to enter, and even my late uncle said, '…that house wasn't right!' Then there are countless smaller experiences, faded with time, each spooky enough on its own, without needing all the other incidents contained herein.

We were paranormally (and permanently) spooked for almost two decades! And yet, even though these events occurred decades ago, between 1965 and 1984, I found that as I spent days and weeks recalling them to write this book, the chills of fear and fright from back then returned more than a few times. In fact, it is still unsettling to think that we actually lived and slept there.

It was one thing to know who or what your tormentor was, but quite another when they lurked surreptitiously in the shadows of the paranormal, simply watching and waiting, as if you were their prey. To be malevolently toyed with at their discretion was terrifying. They acted with the assumed knowledge that their actions were beyond the reach of our reflective intimidation or retribution. That was the true horror.

My mother tried so desperately to move us. We spoke to many people who wanted to exchange properties, but every single one fell through. It seemed we were doomed to live there in existential perpetuity! Then, some new houses were built nearby, and we finally moved to a smaller, much smaller, home. After years of searching, and finding absolutely no takers, we were at last on our way.

And yet, the house—with all its cognitive influences and eerie manifestations that had haunted us for nearly two decades—had one final 'special' in store. This last act pushed us to the brink of madness, plunging us into despair, and leaving us in abject tears of discombobulation.

As I said, my mother looked and looked, and so did I, for a house exchange. With no internet back then, we made countless telephone calls, wrote letters, and placed endless postcards in local shop windows advertising for an exchange—I even travelled to other areas to post them myself. We regularly visited the local council offices to check the exchange book for new listings. Our search was not limited to local exchanges; we considered, even if only within reason, national options as well. In short, we were utterly exhausted from trying, and when you factor in the toll of simply living in that house, it is no surprise we felt constantly drained.

On the day of the move, while our possessions were being slowly but surely loaded onto the removal van, one of our friendly neighbours—who had moved in around the same time as my parents—walked across the road and asked if he could have something of ours. I said, 'yes,' and carried it over to him. While there, we walked around his house and chatted about our move.

'I didn't know you wanted to move,' he said.

I was surprised by his comment, as he had always been so close to us. Then again, we had tried to keep all house activity—and even our efforts to arrange an exchange—as quiet as possible, given everything that had happened there. We briefly spoke about this, and to my surprise, he seemed to know about the activity, at least in part.

'It wouldn't bother me, I'm totally unreceptive to that!' he opined with great confidence.

'So much has gone on—that's why we need to get out!' I replied honestly. After all, what could happen now? We were on our way, thankfully. Little did I know what was to follow shortly.

You have a lovely house,' I continued, adding that it was exactly the kind of house my mother had always wanted, but never had: a kitchen at the front; a long lounge stretching across the back with patio doors; and a back garden that sloped away from the house, unlike ours, which sloped towards it.

He then said something that, to this day, seems incredible, given all the hard work and endless hours we had invested in achieving a house exchange over fifteen years or more.

As he stood on his landing, watching the removal people slowly transfer our possessions—and memories—out of our house, he spoke nonchalantly, seemingly unaware of the immense impact his words would have on me in the next few seconds:

'I've always loved your house and would have exchanged with you, just like that, had you asked!'

In an instant, his statement hurled me from abnegation to stark realisation. If you've ever felt as though the world had opened up beneath you, you will understand this moment. All your aspirations, hopes, and dreams seemed to tumble into a pit of unwarranted, pernicious abandonment. Without the slightest understanding, he had shattered everything that had justified our move. It was as if all of it had been reduced to a million fractured pieces.

'What!' I shouted, without meaning to.

'Really!' I added, my stupefaction palpable.

'Oh my God! You're telling me that after years and years of trying to move—and being singularly unsuccessful—you were here all the time, just twenty yards across the road from us!' I said so rapidly that even I felt impressed, if undeservedly so.

'Yes. I didn't know you wanted to move!' he quickly replied, seemingly sensing the sheer consternation I felt at the situation and the sudden personal revelation it had thrust upon me.

A thousand thoughts ran through my mind. Could I stop the move? Would he consider our new house instead?

'Oh, what the hell is going on!' I asked him to come across and tell my mother what he had just said. He declined, so it was left to me to deliver the news. My mother took it very badly and stormed off to see if anything could be salvaged. Nothing came of the chat, and we were soon on our way.

I can't say for certain that the house's weirdness caused this, but the entire situation felt utterly bizarre—almost as if guided by an orchestration both fate-like and unknown. For 20 years, we had searched for an exchange house without success.

Yet, long after we had moved, another neighbour revealed something extraordinary: the very neighbour who had wanted our house had assumed we ourselves wanted to leave the area, which was why he never approached us. Adding to the strangeness, my father had played snooker with this same neighbour twice a week at a local club years before the move. Yet he had never clarified the type of house we were seeking. Countless other house-moving plans had gone awry, sometimes inexplicably, reinforcing the sense that ordinary logic could not fully explain what was happening.

The mystery deepened. In every other failed exchange, people who had desperately wanted our house turned away the moment they stepped inside. This happened even though it matched exactly what they had said they were looking for. Each sudden change of heart felt less like chance and more like some unseen hand. This hand was deliberate, subtle, and almost mischievous, guiding events according to its own inscrutable design.

And then, if fate—or the house itself—was to play its final move with immaculate timing, it did so perfectly. I could not have made this up—not that I have to.

Had we known about the neighbour's mistaken assumption, this book might never have existed.

A weighty realisation. One that left me aghast at the enormity of it all.

Chapter Ten

The Nineteen-Year Ordeal: A Review of the House's Paranormal Warfare

Having now recounted, as memory allows, a retrospective account of our paranormal experiences of *The Unknown* in our house, I believe you may agree that what we encountered transcends mere folklore. It was a consistent and sustained demonstration of a powerful, active, non-physical intelligence, ever-present and watchful, focused entirely on our house and on us. Its intentions were otherworldly, its presence inescapable, and its awareness of every movement, every sound, undeniable.

The sheer volume of incidents throughout those nineteen years showed an entity with a clear paranormal inclination to interact with, and often control, its environment. You read of its substantial energy, which was proven not by vague shadows.

The force was so great that it sent a heavy cylinder hoover flying five feet across the hallway, striking and damaging the door. It could bang a tray out of hands. These acts, alongside the movement of dressing-table drawers that were shifted without human touch, proved that we were dealing with more than just a lingering presence.

The manifestations were highly invasive and deeply personal. They were designed to torment us in our most vulnerable moments, especially while we lay in bed.

The entity moved from merely displacing objects to making direct, chilling contact.

At night, we felt knocking at the foot of the bed and sensed something heavy perching on the edge of the mattress. Sheets were yanked down without warning, and a cold, unseen finger traced my limbs, leaving me almost paralysed with terror. This compounded the knowledge that it had made my brother so fearful he was driven from the room. We also saw its raw kinetic power outside of the bedroom, such as when the tray was violently banged out of my hands.

The very heart of the house's malevolence was the back bedroom, which clearly acted as a psychic nexus. This was evident when it caused my stoic uncle and aunt to flee after they saw two figures and the curtains appear to be ablaze within the room.

This pervasive focus on danger was further demonstrated through the entity's subtle but persistent interference with the house's core functions. It aligned with the threats posed by the heating and gas supplies. This intelligence drew on power to cause the rapid drainage of batteries and led to inexplicable systemic failures across the house.

Safety, however, was compromised far beyond electrical issues; it was perpetually threatened at a structural level. The house's inherent vulnerability became undeniable with the discovery of the gas main dent. This dent, years-old and present since my parents moved in, revealed a profound and persistent risk embedded within the very structure of the building.

Yet, the conflict was not one-sided: a period of respite occurred after the involvement of the church, which led to a noticeable diminishing of the activity. Sadly, this relief was

101

temporary, and the entity returned with its full malicious force, continuing the ordeal for years.

This existence was marked by a haunting duality in the non-physical realm. While the house's malevolent presence seemed determined to provoke fear, anxiety, or harm, an unseen benevolent force also intervened. In the chapter 'Saved By An Angel,' I describe how an unknown presence physically hurled me to safety during a violent incident involving my brother. This protective intervention profoundly shaped my daily life during that time, and indeed, the life of my family. Perhaps this protective shield was present across many of our encounters, quietly preventing our experiences from becoming far worse.

Perhaps the most confusing, yet compelling, evidence of its presence was the barrage of false sensory data. We were constantly subjected to auditory illusions, such as the convincing sound of the front door slamming or the clicking of high heels on the path.

Most notably, we saw ghosts walk past our kitchen window. This was accompanied by the distinct crunching sound of footsteps on our side path, even though the actual surface was concrete pavement. This was an entity that controlled what we saw and heard, keeping us isolated and perpetually on edge.

Finally, the ultimate confirmation of this entity's manipulative power was the way it directly impacted our emotional and physical state. The spirit fights in my sleep left me physically exhausted, and the deep, unexplained breathing suggested a malignant sentience always nearby.

The trauma reached its peak with the bizarre communication failures that blocked our escape, leaving us isolated and vulnerable. It became terrifyingly clear that this was no ordinary haunting. It was a presence intent not merely on frightening us, but on keeping us captive, under its relentless, unseen control. And if this was not bad enough, other episodes have faded in the years since, yet I know there were more.

The house, through all these phenomena, made its malicious, intelligent, and unequivocally unknown nature profoundly clear.

***

Printed in Dunstable, United Kingdom

71148187R00068